MW00891905

THE STORY OF THE PRAYER SHAWL

The Teaching Tool Sent By God As Seen In Scripture And Modern History

COPYRIGHT 2016

LIFETOUCHING MINISTRIES

1660 River Road Unit 19, Marysville, Mi 48040

All rights reserved. This book is protected by the copyright laws of the United States of America. This book may not be copied or reprinted for commercial gain or profit. The use of short quotations or occasional page copying for personal or group study is permitted and encouraged. Permission will be granted upon request.

Unless otherwise identified, Scripture quotations are taken from the New King James Version®. Copyright © 1982 by Thomas Nelson. Used by permission. All rights reserved.

All emphasis within Scripture quotations is the author's own.

Table of Contents

Acknowledgments
And Dedication

Without reservation, I am able to say that if it was not for my wonderful wife, Margi and my daughter-in-law Julie Bambusch this book would not have been written. I had intended on writing a completely different book and had already started on it.

While visiting our son Butch and his wife Julie Bambusch we saw the prayer shawls that Julie was making for people in her church. When we returned home, my wife Margi began making prayer shawls herself. Soon people began to ask what the tassels and the prayer shawl meant. I was even asked why I was wearing one when I came to church.

It became obvious to us that if people were ever to appreciate what was being given to them they would need some understanding. I wrote a small note card that gave a brief explanation, but my wife began to press me to write this book.

Eventually, I acquiesced to her promptings and put my other book on the back burner. At first, I thought I would be fortunate to have 75 to 100 pages. However, as I began to put the material together it rapidly grew into a major work.

I appreciate greatly the encouragement from Butch and Julie. They have provided various insights which has expanded my original understanding of this subject. When it comes to Hebraic roots, we feed off each other and stimulate each other's thinking.

My wife, Margi, has always been eager to hear me read each chapter when I finished writing it. We have shared many a wonderful time together praising the Lord for what He was revealing.

Therefore, it is only fitting that I dedicate this book to my wife Margi, our son Butch and his wife Julie. I appreciate so much all they have done to make this book what it is.

I also want to dedicate this book to all who are ardent pursuers of our Lord and Savior. Those who understand the Jewishness of our Master. Those who want to know more about this Jewish man who came, died, and rose again; this Jewish man who was God in the flesh.

Preface

Psalms 61:4 *"I long to dwell in your tent* (prayer shawl) *forever and take refuge in the shelter of your wings* (tassels).*"*

After reading the pages in this book, I believe you will also echo King David's sentiments recorded above. You are about to encounter a teaching tool like no other! This is A Teaching Tool Sent By God.

The prayer shawl, although perceived to be Jewish, does not belong to the Jews. It belongs to Heaven! The idea for this garment originated with God Himself! Therefore, the prayer shawl with the attached tassels, belongs to the Kingdom of Heaven. Anything that comes from the Kingdom of Heaven belongs to everybody. The teaching that this garment provides belongs to every man, woman, and child who is alive on this planet.

If the enemy can make this garment Jewish, then he can make it a target for antisemitism. The root of all racism is a hatred of God. Because men hate God they hate who God loves, and God loves the Jews!

The Jews have been hated longer than any other people group. In fact, the reason the Christian church does not know its Hebraic roots is because antisemitism is alive within its systems. Ever since 313 A.D., Christianity has systematically removed Jewish influences out of our churches, our Bibles, our holidays, and ultimately out of our lives.

This book is an attempt by the author to restore to the church one aspect of our lost Hebraic roots. It is my prayer that you will read it slowly and meditatively in order to allow Holy Spirit to speak to you through these pages.

The prayer shawl is a teaching tool sent by God. It is an object lesson where God can educate us about Himself. Education in the things of God brings direction in our lives. This direction, when followed, brings peace and promotion. The prayer shawl literally drapes a story over your heart and lungs.

You will no doubt notice that I have not capitalized satan in this book. I do this for two reasons. First of all, satan is not a name, satan literally means "enemy" or "adversary". As such, satan is simply a descriptive name of an unnamed being. He does not deserve a name.

The second reason is because I do not want to, even for one moment, legitimize his existence by capitalizing as one would a proper name. Only when satan begins a sentence will you ever see the word satan capitalized.

You will also notice that I use the word Yeshua throughout this text. Yeshua is the Hebrew name for Jesus. I am not opposed to the name Jesus and I use this name frequently in my daily life. However, I feel it is necessary for us Gentiles to become acquainted with the Jewish form of His name. As you will find while reading this book, God has intended for Jews and Gentiles to worship together as "one new man". We need to be prepared to share our love for Yeshua with our Jewish friends. By doing so will go a long way in breaking down the wall of separation that has been built between Jew and Gentile.

There are also a few Hebrew names for God throughout the book. I prefer to refer to the Hebrew names because they are more precise and offer a different aspect of who God is. The main names used are the following:

Elohim – In your Bibles, wherever you see the word "God" it is a translation of this Hebrew word. This word describes God as Creator and Judge of the universe. It is the plural form of Eloah which means "powerful, mighty One" which appears 70 times in the O.T. and is translated God as well.

Yahweh – In your Bibles, wherever you see the word "LORD" in all caps it is a translation of this Hebrew word. This word describes God as the Deliverer of His covenant people. The basic difference between Elohim and Yahweh is that Elohim is used when His creation is in need of a judge. Yahweh is used when His creation is in need of His mercy.

Yahweh is also written in Hebrew with four letters often called the tetragrammation. These letters are יהוה. In English this would be YHVH. Since we have changed the "Y" sound to a "J" sound over the centuries, you can see that we have come to say Jehovah for this name. No one knows the correct pronunciation for this name, we simply make our best guess with the information we have available.

Adonai – In your Bibles, wherever you see the word "Lord", with only the first letter capitalized, it is a translation of this Hebrew word. This word describes God as "Master" or "Ruler". Because Jewish people revere the name of Yahweh so greatly they refuse to say the name. They will substitute Adonai for Yahweh or they will simply say "HaShem", which means "The Name".

HaMaschiach – In your Bibles, wherever you see the word "Christ" it is a translation of this Hebrew word. It means "The Messiah", or "The Anointed One". He is the ultimate Deliverer who will restore all that was lost in the fall.

In writing this book it was impossible to write about every single time the prayer shawl was connected in some way. As you read your Bible with fresh Hebrew eyes, I am sure that Holy Spirit will show you many places where the prayer shawl is connected. I want to encourage you to explore your personal interpretations as Holy Spirit leads. However, I encourage you to research your discoveries so that you do not read into the Word of God that which is not there.

I have omitted the event where Jesus went to the home of Jairus and raised his daughter from the dead (Mark 5:41). In this passage, Jesus is recorded as saying "Talitha Cumi". The writer then translates this Aramaic term as "Damsel arise". There are some very respected Bible scholars who put forth the idea that Jesus was actually saying "girl under the tallit arise". They suggest that the Jewish scribes made an error in copying this phrase.

Since "tallit" is the Hebrew word for "prayer shawl", they conclude that the girl was either under her own prayer shawl or under the prayer shawl of Jesus.

I have great difficulty in agreeing with this conclusion for at least two reasons.

1. In Mark, there are two other occasions where the author gave the interpretation for an Aramaic expression. In Mark 7:34 he used the Aramaic "ephphatha" and then translated it "be opened". In Mark 15: 34-36 Jesus says "Eloi Eloi lama sabachthani" and the writer translates this as "My God, My God,

10

why have you forsaken me?" If a copyist made an error in the account of Jairus' daughter then how can we trust these in text translations of Aramaic, let alone the rest of the Bible.

2. In Acts 9:40, Peter said to Dorcas, "Tabitha arise". There is only one letter difference between Peter's words and Jesus' words over Jairus' daughter. If "Talitha Cumi" is talking about a prayer shawl, then we might also make this say the same thing. Those that believe the tallit was the word in question with the raising of Jairus' daughter do not connect the raising of Dorcas to the same garment.

I purposefully left out personal stories. I am aware that books today appeal to readers through that method of writing. However, I wanted to allow the Scripture to speak to you individually without being guided to a particular conclusion through a personal application of my life. It is my hope that you will experience many life changing moments as you read this book. I believe the telling of the stories within the Word of God has an ability to speak to people more effectively than my own personal experiences ever would. Besides, my experiences are not the standard, the Word of God is the standard.

You will find that this is not a book which you can read quickly. I encourage you to take your time. Allow Holy Spirit to stop your reading from time to time so you can ruminate on what you have read. Let the teachings within this wonderful teaching tool change your life.

It is my hope that you will experience at least some of the life changing moments that I experienced as I wrote this book. Writing this book has had a profound affect upon my life. I believe it will have the same on yours as well.

May the Lord bless you as you begin your education inside the pages of this book.

Chapter One
Introduction

The garment that has become known as the Jewish prayer shawl has interesting Biblical significance. Before we get into the various Biblical references, let us begin by describing this garment in detail. The prayer shawl is best understood by its Hebrew name, טילת (tallit). This word is pronounced tah-leet'. The word tallit is formed by two words "tal"(meaning tent) and "lith" (meaning little). Therefore, this would make the tallit (or prayer shawl) a little tent.

Literally, then, every person has his or her own "tent of meeting". Six million Jews could not fit into the Tent of Meeting or Tabernacle of Moses. Therefore, God gave them their own private Sanctuary where they could meet with God. This was their Prayer Closet. As we continue in our study, we will find how this is significant to us.

Even today, the Jewish people say that the Prayer Shawl is a religious symbol which envelops the Jew both physically and spiritually, in prayer and celebration, in joy and sorrow. It is used for all major Jewish occasions: Circumcision, Bar Mitzvahs, Weddings, and Burials. It protects the scrolls of the Torah when they are moved. The dead are wrapped in it when they are buried. The Bride and Groom are covered with the canopy of the Prayer Shawl. It inspired the Jewish Flag!

The tallit only serves to provide for the tassels that are attached to the four corners. These tassels are called tzitzit (tzeet-zeet) in Hebrew. The word tzitzit is written in Hebrew as ציצית. The tallit is an ordinary garment until the tassels are put on. The tassels or tzitzit then make the tallit a holy garment.

Before the Babylonian Captivity, the tallit was a rectangular mantel that looked like a poncho with an opening for the head to go through. After the Babylonian captivity, the garment gradually evolved into the prayer shawl that we see today.

Initially, the tallit was worn daily, as part of the clothing, but after the exile of the Jews from the land of Israel and their dispersion, they came to adopt the fashions of their gentile neighbors and the tallit became a religious garment for prayer; hence, it is now referred to as a Prayer Shawl.

Let's look at the Prayer shawl.

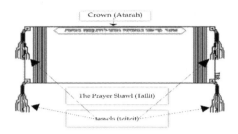

The first thing we will look at is the Crown, or Atarah (עטרה). This is pronounced ah-tah-rah'. There are Hebrew words written here. These Hebrew words are: (reading right to left)

"בָּרוּךְ אַתָּה יהוה אלהנו מלך העולם אשר קדשנו
במצותיו וצונו להתעטף בציצית"

(Transliteration) "ba-rukh' at-tah' Yah'-way, E-lo-hay'-nu Me-lekh' ha-o-lam' a-sher' kid-de-shay'-nu be-mits'-vo-tav ve-tsi'-va-nu le-hit'-ah-teif ba-tzit'-tzit."

(Translation) "Blessed are you, Yahweh, our Elohim, Ruler of the Universe, who makes us holy with his mitzvot, and told us to enwrap ourselves in tzitzit. "

This is the prayer that a Jew says when he is getting ready to put on the tallit (prayer shawl). The mitzvot (commandment) that this prayer refers to is in Numbers 15:37-41.

Then he would quote Psalms 104:1-2

"Bless the LORD, O my soul! O LORD my God, You are very great: You are clothed with honor and majesty, who cover Yourself with light as with a garment, who stretch out the heavens like a curtain."

17

In the Jewish mind, it is understood that they are imitating God who clothes Himself with light as with a garment when they are putting on the Prayer Shawl. They are entering into the Light with God.

This brings to mind a New Testament scripture:

1 John 1:7 *"But if we walk in the light, as he is in the light, we have fellowship one with another, and the blood of Jesus Christ his Son cleanses us from all sin."*

Already we are beginning to see how this garment played such an important part not only in the Old Testament but also in the New Testament saint's lives. It is obvious that John got the concept of walking in the light from wearing the prayer shawl. John took the physical wearing of the prayer shawl and shows us the spiritual application to our lives.

In Jewish thinking, this reference to God clothing Himself with light as with a garment would hark back to the beginning. In Genesis 1:4 it says *"God saw **the light** and it was good."* This light lights every man in this world. (John 1:9). Also in Revelation 21:3, it states that the Lamb is the light. In Hebrew the words "the light" in Genesis 1:4 is האור את (et-ha'-or).

In Hebrew, each letter also represents a number. It is a long-standing study within Judaism that equates the numerical value of each letter to an esoteric meaning.

Looking at the following chart of numerical values for the Hebrew letters, we find the following amazing connection:

א = 1

ת = 400

ה = 5

א = 1

ו = 6

ר = 200

1	א	10	י	100	ק
2	ב	20	כ	200	ר
3	ג	30	ל	300	ש
4	ד	40	מ	400	ת
5	ה	50	נ		
6	ו	60	ס		
7	ז	70	ע		
8	ח	80	פ		
9	ט	90	צ		

When this is totaled, you arrive at the number 613, the number of commandments in the Mosaic Law. Thus, then, "the light" corresponds to the full number of commandments in the Law. We recognize that Yeshua (Jesus) kept every commandment of the Law perfectly. With this understanding, we can connect walking in the light with walking in the commandments. Therefore, I John 1:7 could be understood as follows:

"But if we walk in obedience to His commandments, as he has walked in obedience to the commandments, we have fellowship one with another, and the blood of Jesus Christ his Son cleanses us from all sin."

This would help us to realize that the fellowship with Him, as well as continual cleansing from all sin, is contingent on us walking in the light (i.e. Keeping His commandments). In fact, Yeshua said the same thing, in as many words, in John 14:15: *"If you love me, keep my commandments"*. Moreover, He continues His thought in verse 23. *"If a man love me, he will keep my words; and my Father will love him, and we will come unto him, and make our abode with him."* This sounds very similar to "walking in the light ", doesn't it?

Isn't it amazing at how much richer the Word of God becomes with just a little knowledge of our Hebrew roots? Can you imagine how much more we would learn if we made learning our Hebrew heritage a lifelong quest?

You may be familiar with the term Bar Mitzvah. This is a

Hebrew term that is written as בר מעוה **. . .** "Bar" is Aramaic for "son of" and "Mitzvah" means "Law or commandment". Hence, "Bar Mitzvah" means "Son of the Law". This takes place at age 13 for boys and 12 for girls. At a child's Bar Mitzvah (Bat Mitzvah if a girl), they are presented with their first Prayer Shawl. They are now considered personally responsible to the Law (Torah). The Prayer Shawl, with its attached tzitzits, serve as a reminder of their obligation to walk circumspectly within the teachings of the Bible.

The Prayer Shawl holds a mystery that will unlock the Word of God for us. In order for us to understand all that this Prayer Shawl holds for us, we must first have some basic teaching.

Numbers have theological importance in Christianity. They have even more so in Judaism. Therefore, a basic understanding of numerology is necessary if we are to begin to unravel the mystery that is held within the Prayer Shawl.

God reveals through Numbers

One is the number of God, the beginning, source, commencement, first. One is the number of compound unity. One is a numerical number as in, only One.

Two is the number of witness or testimony. Two is also the number of division or separation.

Three is the number of the Godhead. Three is the number of Divine completeness and perfect testimony.

Four is the number of earth, creation, world. We experience four seasons, four winds, four corners of the earth.

Five is the number of the cross, grace, atonement, life. There are five offerings in the Tabernacle of Moses. There are the five wounds of Yeshua on the cross.

Six is the number of man. Man is to labor six days and rest one. Man was created on the sixth day.

Seven is the number of spiritual completion and perfection. The Israelites marched around Jericho seven times. Yeshua shed His blood seven times during the entire process of his beatings, torture, and ultimate crucifixion.

Eight is the number of resurrection, a new beginning. Noah was the eighth person from creation and the flood brought about a new beginning on the earth.

Twelve is the number of divine government and apostolic fullness. There are twelve apostles of the Lamb.

Thirty is the number of mourning and grief. Aaron's death was mourned for thirty days. Moses' death was mourned for thirty days. Judas sold Yeshua for thirty pieces of silver and then was sorry and threw the money on the floor in front of the chief priest and elders.

Forty is the number of testing, trial, or probation. It also indicates transition or change. The Israelites wandered 40 years in the wilderness. Yeshua was tested for 40 days in the desert.

666 is the number of the antichrist

God reveals through colors

In addition to numbers, colors also have theological implications as well. Gold signifies Deity. Silver signifies Redemption. Brass signifies Judgment. Blue is the color that represents Heavenly Origin. Purple represents Royalty and Kingship. Scarlet demonstrates Sacrifice. The color white represents purity and sinless humanity.

In the next chapter, we will be looking at one particular color that God uses to reveal Himself in this Prayer Shawl. That color is the color blue or as it is called in the Hebrew Bible, Tekhelet (תכלת).

Now that we have a foundation for our study of the prayer shawl, let us begin by looking at the tzitzit (tassels). The Scripture that begins our discovery of the hidden mysteries of the tzitzit and ultimately the prayer shawl is Numbers 15:37-41.

"Again the LORD spoke to Moses, saying, "Speak to the children of Israel: Tell them to make tassels on the corners of their garments throughout their generations, and to put a blue thread in the tassels of the corners. And you shall have the tassel, that you may look upon it and remember all the commandments of the LORD, and do them, and that you may not follow the harlotry to which your own heart and your own eyes are inclined, and that you may remember and do all My commandments, and be holy for your God. I am the LORD your God, who brought you out of the land of Egypt, to be your God: I am the LORD your God."

Two things are notable here: tassels (Tzitzit) and blue thread (Tekhelet). We will start by considering what the tzitzit represent.

The cause given for the tzitzit is that "they may look upon it and recall all the commandments of the LORD, and do them". The pronoun "it" in this verse in the masculine, not neuter. Actually, the verse should read (with a masculine pronoun), *"they may look upon **Him** and remember all the commandments of the LORD and do them"*.

The tzitzit was more than a colored string. The tzitzit was a picture of One who was to come. The tzitzit was Him (the Messiah). This reality will become more vivid as we delve into the mysteries within this study.

The reason for God giving this commandment to the children of Israel is explained in the previous verses of Numbers 15:32-36.

"Now while the children of Israel were in the wilderness, they found a man gathering sticks on the Sabbath day. And those who found him gathering sticks brought him to Moses and Aaron, and to all the congregation. They put him under guard, because it had not been explained what should be done to him. Then the LORD said to Moses, "The man must surely be put to death; all the congregation shall stone him with stones outside the camp." So, as the LORD commanded Moses, all the congregation brought him outside the camp and stoned him with stones, and he died."

At first glimpse, this punishment seems extreme in our Western thinking. As we see deeper into the actions of this man, we will realize the justness of the penalty.

God had delivered the Israelites out of Egypt. He brought them to Mount Sinai and had given them the 10 commandments. God had commanded Moses to build a Tabernacle (a tent of meeting) for His Presence to abide in the midst of them. God was their King and they were His servants. One of the 10 commandments was to hallow the Sabbath day. They were to do no work. God was providing manna for them and on the 6th day, they were to gather twice as much manna and cook it before the Sabbath. There would be no manna from heaven on the Sabbath.

A man was gathering sticks on the Sabbath. There would have been only two reasons that anyone would need to be gathering sticks. One is to make a fire for cooking and two, to make a fire for warmth.

He did not need the sticks to cook food for his family because Manna would have spoiled if it were not cooked on the day before the Sabbath. Manna fell from heaven every day except the Sabbath. They would gather what they needed for their family for each day. On the day before the Sabbath, they were to gather twice as much for their family and cook it before the Sabbath began.

He did not need to gather sticks to build a fire for warmth because they were in the desert and no same person would start a fire unnecessarily.

It is plain to see that his object in gathering the sticks was simply to show, openly and publicly with a high hand, that he despised God his King, and refused to obey His holy ordinance. He had essentially set himself apart from every other Israeli and declared, by his actions, that he could make his own rules and did not need God to tell him what to do. However, he was not defying an earthly king. He was defying the King of kings and LORD of lords!

Israel was being ruled by a Theocracy. This was not a Democracy, a Monarchy, or even an Oligarchy. His actions, if allowed, would start Anarchy among this newly formed Nation. This Nation would bring the Messiah. This Nation would make it possible for mankind to be redeemed from the fall of Adam. The stakes were too high for God to ignore. Man's salvation was at stake. Rightly, therefore, that man was put to death.

God realized that the children of Israel needed more than a law. They needed more than a tabernacle. They needed something that they could see every day, all day long, to remind them of His commandments. They needed a teaching tool that would constantly remind them of what God required of them. They needed their own personal "tent of meeting" where they could meet with God individually.

God told Moses to have the people put tassels on each of the four corners of their garments. On one of the strings on each tassel would be the color Tekhelet (blue). This would provide Moses a teaching tool to tell the Israelites not only about the Law but also about the coming Messiah.

Let's look at how that teaching would have been accomplished by examining the tzitzit itself.

The Hebrew word for tzitzit is ציצת. Looking again at the chart for the numerical values of the letters, we see that the four Hebrew letters that make up the word tzitzit equals 600.

23

צ = 90

י = 10

צ = 90

י = 10

ת = 400

The eleventh-century Biblical commentator, Rashi, explains how looking at the tassels reminds one of all God's commandments. "The word tzitzit (tassels) is numerically equivalent to 600. Tzitzit are traditionally tied with eight strings and five knots. 600 + 8 + 5 = 613, which is the number of commandments in the Torah. Linguistically, however, the subject of the sentence (that which is to remind us of God's commandments) is not the tzitzit, but rather the thread of blue (the tekhelet)."

Therefore, when one would look at the tzitzit, they would be reminded of the Torah. They would remember the commandments of Yahweh. Not only would these remind the wearer of the Torah, but it would also be a testimony to others that the one wearing the tzitzit was held to a higher standard of conduct. Therefore, the one wearing the tzitzit would not want to be embarrassed by someone observing him not obeying God's teaching.

Furthermore, the tzitzit consists of eight dangling threads (4 threads doubled over). One of those eight threads is the color Tekhelet (Royal Blue). This thread is called the Shemosh, which means servant. The royal blue signifies Kingship. Therefore, this ribbon of blue speaks of the Servant – King, who is the Jewish Messiah. Jesus (Yeshua), came as a servant to mankind. However, He is returning as King of kings and LORD of lords! Yeshua is our Servant-King. He is what is pictured by the Shemosh.

There are 5 knots tied at various intervals. Beginning with a knot, then 7 windings and a knot, then 8 windings and a knot, then 11 windings and a knot, then 13 windings and a knot. The knots represent the 5 books of Moses (Torah). When a Jewish person would touch or look at the 5 knots, they would be reminded of the mitzvots (commandments) that God gave them on Mount Sinai.

Not only would they remember the commandments, when they looked on the tzitzit they would also remember "Him" (the Messiah). Let's look again at Numbers 15:37-41.

"Again the LORD spoke to Moses, saying, "Speak to the children of Israel: Tell them to make tassels on the corners of their garments throughout their generations, and to put a blue thread in the tassels of the corners. And you shall have the tassel, that you may look upon it and remember all the commandments of the LORD and do them, and that you may not follow the harlotry to which your own heart and your own eyes are inclined, and that you may remember and do all My commandments, and be holy for your God. I am the LORD your God, who brought you out of the land of Egypt, to be your God: I am the LORD your God."

Here is an amazing thing that appears only in the Hebrew. The word that is translated "it" ("*that you may look upon it*") in our King James English Bibles and understood by the Jewish people as "Him" is written אתו. The vav (ו) in ancient Hebrew was a picture of a nail and meant, among other things, connection, piercing, fastening, etc. The other two letters in this word is a word that is not translatable. The only thing that the Jewish linguists say about this word is that it is a direct object pointer. This is a misfortunate conclusion that is not consistent with the language of the Hebrew Bible. Sometimes it is present, while at other times it is not present even when speaking about the same direct object.

So, then, there must be a different explanation for this "untranslatable" word. The word is spelled with two letters, the Aleph, and the Tav. These two letters are the first and the last letters of the Hebrew alphabet. In English, we would say the A and the Z. In Greek, we would say the Alpha and the Omega. That should remind you of what Yeshua said in Revelation, "I am the Alpha and Omega". Yeshua reveals to John, a Jewish man who knew about this mysterious "untranslatable" word, that He (Yeshua) is that word! What John had been looking at all his life when he looked on his tzitzit and saw "Him", he was seeing Yeshua the Messiah!

When you look at the word אתו you see the meaning "the Aleph Tav that was pierced"! Hebrew is amazing! There is so much hidden in plain sight all through the Hebrew text! So, then, the Scripture would read (with our new understanding) in Numbers 15:39

*"And you shall have the tassel, that you may look upon **the Aleph Tav that was pierced** and remember all the commandments of the LORD and do them...*

Therefore, by the blue thread alone they would "remember the commandments and do them". The blue thread, even without the knots, would have been enough of a reason to keep the commandment.

How about us? Is it enough for us to look upon Calvary, upon the Aleph Tav that was pierced, and keep His commandments?

Hebrews 12:1b-2 *"let us lay aside every weight, and the sin which so easily ensnares us, and let us run with endurance the race that is set before us, looking unto Jesus, the author and finisher of our faith, who for the joy that was set before Him endured the cross, despising the shame, and has sat down at the right hand of the throne of God."*

The word tallit (טילת) in ancient Hebrew (as Moses would have originally written the word) would have been printed like this: +∠ᴗ⊕.

Hebrew began as a picture language. Each letter was a picture. During the Babylonian captivity, the letters began to be written more in line with what we see in Hebrew today.

When an ancient Hebrew wanted to create a new word, he (or she) would go through a painstaking process in which to describe the action (not the appearance) of the object. They would find individual pictographs that "told the story", so to speak, of the object. Once done, they would then work out the pronunciation.

So, what is "the story" behind the word tallit? The four pictographs, that later became Hebrew letters are ⊕ (tet), ᴗ (yod), ∠ (lamed), + (tav). Tet means to surround or coil. Yod means right hand of power or strength. Lamed means shepherd, authority, or instruction. Tav means covenant and is in the shape of a cross. The "story" of the action expected by one who wears the tallit would be this: "To surround with the strength, power, authority, and teaching of the covenant of the cross."

When you finish this book, you will see just how much the tallit teaches us about the covenant of the cross. How amazing it is that Moses would use the tallit to give such a deep revelation to the children of Israel. We can still benefit from learning about the teachings of the tallit. This fact alone makes one want to purchase a tallit and wear it proudly even today!

The exercise of tying the tzitzit is an educational process in itself. While twisting, wrapping, and knotting the strings together, one is reminded of the Scripture in Isaiah 40:31.

"But they that wait upon the LORD shall renew their strength; they shall mount up with wings as eagles; they shall run, and not be weary; and they shall walk, and not faint."

The word "wait" in this verse is the Hebrew קָוָה. This is pronounced (Kah-vah'). This word means (among other things) to twist and bind as a rope. So, if we were to read this with the understanding of twisting and tying the tzitzit, we would have the following expanded thought:

"Those who want to be successful in their relationship with God, mounting up with wings as eagles, will make a spiritual tzitzit by twisting, tying, and binding their lives together with the life of the LORD, thereby gaining the strength they need for successful living."

That is a very different picture of "wait" than we have in our Western thinking. Our view of "wait" is usually passive. This, however, is active. Always remember that the Bible is a Jewish Bible (even the New Testament). The Bible was written by Jews, for Jews, and about the Jewish experience. The more we learn about the deeper meaning of words from a Jewish perspective, the richer our own faith becomes. Looking at Scripture from a western mindset is limiting and may even affect our relationship with our Creator.

The phrase "mounting up with wings as eagles" refers to the corners or wings of the tallit. By twisting, tying, and binding your life with the life of the LORD, you will fly higher than you've ever been!

You will be lifted to a higher spiritual plane. You will accomplish more, do more, experience more, than you would without Him.

The next teaching that the tzitzit offers us is the number of the windings of the shemosh (or blue servant thread). There are four groups of windings between each of the five knots. They are 7, 8, 11, and 13. Looking at the Hebrew letter chart again we will uncover this wonderful teaching.

The first three sets of windings (7, 8, and 11 windings), when added equal the number 26. This is the numerical value of the following Hebrew word: יהוה

י = 10

ה = 5

ו = 6

ה = 5

This word is the sacred name of God given to Moses in Exodus 3:13-15. It is transliterated into English as Y H V H. You probably have been told to pronounce this name as Jehovah. Another pronunciation would be Yahweh. In the KJV Bible, this word is translated as I AM. Yeshua identified Himself as the I AM of the Old Testament.

There are 13 windings in the last set. This is the numerical value of the word echad (אחד).

א = 1

ח = 8

ד = 4

Echad (eh-kahd′) is Hebrew for one in unity. When you put those two words together you have (from right to left) יהוה אחד (Yahweh echad – The LORD is one). When one would look or touch the tzitzit (tassel) of the tallit (prayer shawl) they would remember that Yahweh is One. This is the verse in Deuteronomy 6:4 *"Hear, O Israel: The LORD our God is one LORD"*. This is what the Jewish people refer to as the shema (sheh-mah′).

28

Next, let's look at the total number of windings. 7+8+11+13= 39. Yeshua took 39 stripes on his back. These stripes were for our healing. Isaiah 53:5 says, *"by His stripes we are healed."* I Peter 2:24 says, *"by whose stripes ye were healed"*. Isaiah is looking forward to a coming event and Peter is looking back at an accomplished event. You are already healed. It is already completed. God can do no more to heal you than He can do to save you. God has done all He can do. Just like salvation, it is up to you to accept what He has done for you. Once you accept His healing, the healing will manifest. The same as when you accepted His gift of salvation, then you were saved. The same faith that saves you will heal you.

Now, you can see that looking at the tzitzit would remind you of the commandments, the five books of Moses, the shema (Jehovah is one), and the promise of the Messiah who is the Aleph and the Tav. Looking at the tzitzit would also remind you to twist and wrap your life around God so that you would be strong. Even beyond that, by looking at the tekhelet color, you would identify yourself with being a priest and a king.

This brings us to the next chapter concerning the tekhelet (Royal blue).

Chapter Two

TEKHELET (ROYAL BLUE)

Before entering into the history of this color, tekhelet, I have a caution to the reader. Tekhelet was a requirement for the Jewish people. Messiah had not come and tekhelet was one of the many teaching tools that Moses used to show what or who Messiah should be. Tekhelet is but the shadow of Yeshua in the Old Testament. Today we have Yeshua, who is the substance of the shadow. You may want to have a personal prayer shawl, and that is perfectly acceptable. Any blue string is fine to use in order to appreciate the meaning that is associated with the prayer shawl. It is unnecessary to follow the stringent rules in order to understand the significance of wearing the prayer shawl.

It is important to understand that the commandment in Numbers 15:38-41 was for the wearer of the garment that held the tzitzit (tassels) to look upon the string of blue (tekhelet) and remember the commandments. The reason given for the tzitzit is that *"they may look upon it and remember all the commandments of the LORD, and do them"*. The word "it" in this verse in the masculine, not neuter. Actually, the verse should read, "they may look upon "**Him**" and remember all the commandments of the LORD and do them". Since the word tzitzit (tassel) is feminine and the word tekhelet (blue) is masculine, the only antecedent possible for "it" (or Him) is tekhelet.

How would tekhelet remind one of the commandments? To this question, we come to the great Rabbi of the Middle Ages, Maimonides. Maimonides (My-mon'-i-deez), whose full name is Rabbi Moshe ben Maimon (he is also known as Rambam which is an acronym of the first letters of his name), explains how the thread of tekhelet reminds one of all the Commandments.

"Rather the remembrance is through the thread of tekhelet.... For the tekhelet is similar to the sea and the sea is similar to the sky and the sky is similar to God's holy throne".

Maimonides' understanding is based on the color of tekhelet. Its depth of color, similar to the seemingly endless sea and sky, reminds the Jew of the Infinite, which brings him to remember all of God's Commandments.

This brings us to a fascinating scientific fact. Our eye perceives color in a complex fashion based on the various wavelengths that strike it. The color of an object is determined by the wavelengths of light that the object emits or reflects. White light, or sunlight, is made up of all the colors in the spectrum. When that broadband light strikes an object, some of the wavelengths are absorbed and some are reflected, giving the object its characteristic color. For example, the element gold absorbs blue light and reflects the rest. When our eye sees all the reflected colors of the spectrum with the blue missing, it perceives the color as gold.

Ultimately, the color we see is completely determined by which colors an object absorbs and which colors are reflected. No two substances have exactly the same color since no two molecules absorb exactly the same wavelengths of light. The precise measurement of which wavelengths (usually given in units of nanometers-nm) a molecule absorbs (its absorption spectrum) is like a fingerprint, a unique way of identifying it.

Tekhelet is produced from a snail found in the Mediterranean called the Murex Trunculus. Scientists studied the properties of different dye molecules obtained from the Murex trunculus snail. They discovered that the tekhelet molecule (indigotin) gets its color from a strong absorption peak centered at exactly 613 nanometers.

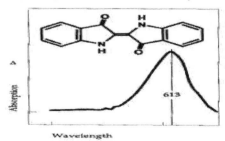

You may recall how that in the last chapter of this book I spoke of the 11th century Rabbi Rashi, who showed that the looking at the tassels reminds one of all God's commandments. "The word tzitzit (tassels) is numerically equivalent to 600. Tzitzit are traditionally tied with eight strings and five knots for a total of 613 (the number of commandments in the Torah).

Another way of understanding the mitzvah (commandment) of tekhelet is based on the association of tekhelet in tzitzit with the tekhelet found in the priestly garments. Tekhelet was part of the priest's clothes and is found in conjunction with the Temple and associated with royalty as well. The priestly garments were also made of wool and linen, a combination usually prohibited in the Torah. The tallit with the tzitzit may also be made of wool and linen and have a thread of tekhelet.

Tekhelet is the epitome of the democratic thrust within Judaism which equalizes not by leveling, but by elevating: all of Israel is enjoined to become a nation of priests. In antiquity, tekhelet was the insignia of authority, high breeding, and nobility. By adding the blue woolen cord to the tzitzit, the Torah combined nobility with priesthood: Israel is not to rule man but to serve God. Furthermore, tekhelet is not restricted to Israel's leaders, be they kings, rabbis or scholars. It is the uniform of all Israel.

The thread of tekhelet was the simple Jew's priestly garb, reminding him that he was indeed a priest and that his responsibilities as such were to keep the Commandments of the Torah.

(Exodus 19:6) "*Now therefore, if you will obey My voice indeed, and keep My covenant, then you shall be My own treasure from among all peoples: for all the earth is Mine: and you shall be to Me a kingdom of priests, and a holy nation.*"

The importance of this thread of tekhelet is discovered within the commandment in Numbers 15. By looking at this thread, the Jewish person would be reminded of all the mitzvahs (commandments). Therefore, the tzitzit represented every one of the mitzvahs that were described by Yahweh Himself! With this information, it is hard to imagine how the Jewish people could ever be without this thread of tekhelet. Yet, they have been without it for over 1300 years! How could this have come about?

To answer this question, we must look at some external as well as some internal conditions that made the disappearance of the tekhelet possible. This also demonstrates how that the revival of the process to produce tekhelet signifies that Yeshua is coming very soon!

36

This reappearance of tekhelet is but one of many events that are exciting to Jew and Christian alike.

In the 13th century the Rambam (Maimonides), in his commentary on the Torah, lamented that *tekhelet* was no longer accessible to Jews:

"And the tekhelet, even today no one would dare wear it other than the king of the gentiles."

In the Bible, tekhelet is usually mentioned together with argaman, the royal purple and tola'at shani (scarlet or crimson). All three appear quite often in the latter part of the book of Exodus, along with the precious materials used in the construction of the Tabernacle and its sacred vessels and garments. Presumably, most of the uses which tekhelet was put in the Tabernacle were then continued in the Temple, when that structure superseded the Tabernacle.

Archeology has found that tekhelet existed as far back as 1750 B.C. in Crete. That would have been almost 50 years after Abraham left the Ur of the Chaldees, to travel to what is today known as Israel. It is entirely likely that the Jewish people would have been able to make this dye within a relatively short time.

Tekhelet is prominent in the O.T. and, as shall be seen in subsequent chapters, is also prominent in the N. T. Because the Second Temple was destroyed in 70 AD, a diminishment of the Jewish tekhelet industry is to be expected, since it was no longer needed for the many uses in that institution. However, the importance of tekhelet for tzitzit, a ritual ornament used in everyday Jewish ritual life, mandated the continued manufacture and distribution of *tekhelet* during the centuries subsequent to the destruction of the Temple.

There were also numerous Roman prohibitions against manufacturing, distributing and even wearing tekhelet, as well as royal purple. Both tekhelet and purple are produced from the same mollusk, in a similar fashion, and with the comparable expense. Both tekhelet and purple were both known as purpura. Both were highly prized, and in Roman times, the wearing of them came to signify high social and legal standing.

In Republican Rome, only the two people who took the census and triumphant generals were permitted to wear clothing dyed completely purple. Consuls and praetors were limited to purple-edged togas and generals on a campaign to a purple cloak.

The use of purple expanded considerably in the Imperial period, and at the same time, there were growing restrictions on its use in the official mode of dress. Beginning in the third century, Roman emperors restricted the manufacture of these dyes to industries owned and operated by the crown, centered in Tyre (in modern-day southern Lebanon). By the late fourth century, an edict in the year 383 A.D. restricted the manufacture and sale of both purpura oxyblatta [argaman – purple] and purpura hyacinthina [tekhelet – blue] solely to the imperial factories.

The legal prohibitions had the effect of making the tekhelet dye a very precious commodity, which might have been, at times, impossible to obtain. Roman rules, however, were notoriously ill-enforced and the effect of any general prohibition depended largely on the local Roman authorities. There is evidence of continued use of tekhelet despite the Roman prohibitions. Even if the Roman prohibitions had an effect in limiting the use of tekhelet among Jews, it seems that this is not what killed the practice.

The Muslim conquest of Palestine and the coastal areas of Lebanon-Syria (in 634 A.D-638 A.D.) brought about an almost total extinction of the imperial dye industry of royal purple and tekhelet-blue. This conquest concluded a 20-year period during which the Jewish population in Palestine endured several massacres by the various factions. This tortured history could not allow for the continuance of tradition.

Then came the final blow to the tekhelet industry. On 9 July A.D. 551 a large earthquake, followed by a tsunami, destroyed most the coastal cities of Phoenicia (modern-day Lebanon). Tripoli is reported to have "drowned," and Beirut did not recover for nearly 1300 years afterward. Geophysical data show this to be one of the most devastating historical submarine earthquakes in the eastern Mediterranean.

This devastating event destroyed the coastal cities in the exact epicenter of the tekhelet industry. It is hard to imagine that it would not have also wiped out the production facilities of purpura dyes in these areas, and probably had a significant direct impact on the mollusk population as well.

These combined factors caused tekhelet to disappear completely. God Himself removed tekhelet because His Son Yeshua was the fulfillment of what this color represented. However, since the Jews are still looking for Messiah and fully expect the temple to be rebuilt, with all the elements of that worship restored, God is bringing back tekhelet in the last days.

In 1913, Rabbi Isaac Herzog wrote a doctoral thesis naming the murex trunculus as the source of the tekhelet dye. This is a picture of the murex trunculus snail.

The problem that faced the Jewish leaders was that the dye from this snail produced purple, not blue. However, in 1980, Professor Otto Elsner of the Shenkar College of Fibers in Israel discovered that when the substance from the glandular secretions of the murex trunculus is exposed to sunlight (i.e. ultraviolet rays) they turn blue.

In 1993, the P'til Tekhelet Foundation was formed in Israel to produce tekhelet strings for tzitzit. They have also worked with The Temple Institute to provide the tekhelet for the High Priests garments as well as the cloth for the 3rd Temple. This provides a vital part of the preparation for the rebuilding of the Temple in our day! This is the fulfillment of prophecy right before our very eyes! Yeshua is coming very soon!

Chapter Three
An Ensign For A Nation

The Jewish prayer shawl inspired the Jewish flag.

As we discover the significance of the Jewish prayer shawl, let us look at the events that fulfilled Biblical prophecy. It was prophesied that God Himself would give them a flag when He caused them to return to their land during the last days. In Isaiah 11:10-12 we read:

*"And in that day **there shall be a Root of Jesse, who shall stand as a banner to the people;** for the Gentiles shall seek Him, and His resting place shall be glorious." It shall come to pass in that day that the LORD shall set His hand again the second time to recover the remnant of His people who are left, from Assyria and Egypt, from Pathros and Cush, from Elam and Shinar, from Hamath and the islands of the sea. **He will set up a banner for the nations,** and will assemble the outcasts of Israel, and gather together the dispersed of Judah from the four corners of the earth."*

It is quite amazing that even with a predominate number of secularists within the Jewish leadership that led to the statehood of Israel in 1948, the flag that was chosen to fly proudly over this restored nation would be patterned after the Jewish prayer shawl! How this came about demonstrates a powerful message to us today.

Amos 9:14-15 says: *"I will bring back the captives of My people Israel; they shall build the waste cities and inhabit them; they shall plant vineyards and drink wine from them; they shall also make gardens and eat fruit from them. I will plant them in their land, and no longer shall they be pulled up from the land I have given them," says the LORD your God."*

Isaiah 11:11 says, *"It shall come to pass in that day that the LORD shall set His hand again the second time **to recover** the remnant of His people who are left…"*

Notice Isaiah uses the word "recover". This signifies that something was lost and needs to be recovered. Isaiah has possession of the land of Israel in mind. However, Israel would not only lose their land, but they would also lose their Hebrew language as well. To "recover" these would take a miracle of Biblical proportions!

It would seem to any logical thinker that such a thing would be an impossibility. No people in history had been conquered and scattered across the face of the earth only to return and restore their national sovereignty after nearly 2000 years. In fact, most Jews had reconciled themselves to the reality that such a restoration could come only when Messiah was revealed. They had resigned themselves to make the best of their situation by assimilating into the nations in which they were dispersed.

The rebirth of Israel actually began many years before 1948. In 1897 the First Zionist Congress was formed. Men of unusual passion arose to insist that both the nation of Israel and the Hebrew language were to be restored so that the Jewish people could have a measure of self-determination and security. Over the subsequent decades, the movement was nurtured by men of the same vision and passion, including Theodor Herzl who championed the cause before governing authorities in the western nations. The recognition that the movement received with the Balfour Declaration in 1917 after such a short time was amazing, despite the fact that early ideas called for establishing a Jewish state in Uganda rather than in the land of Jewish ancestors.

World War I was a significant event in end-time prophecy regarding the regathering of Israel. Turkey, with an expansive empire that compassed the Middle East (including Palestine) and North Africa, fought with Germany and the Central Powers against the Allies. At the breaking up of the Turkish Empire by the victorious Allies, both Jews and Arabs requested independent states. The world powers were generous in the extreme to the Arabs by granting them twenty-two independent Arabs states—encompassing 5,414,000 square miles. The Jews asked for less than one percent of that vast territory. The Allies agreed to this request in the 1917 Balfour Declaration and the 1920 San Remo Conference of World Powers.

However, in 1921 Great Britain reneged on the Balfour Declaration, lopped off 77 percent of the Land promised in the Balfour Declaration, and set up the Arab Emirate of Transjordan. Then in 1922, the League of Nations gave Great Britain a Mandate to prepare the remaining 23 percent of Palestine (including Samaria, Judea, Gaza, Golan Heights and East Jerusalem) for a Jewish National Home. However, under French pressure, in 1923, the Golan Heights was ceded by the British to the French mandate of Syria. They partitioned His Land and the LORD was angry.

Today we are still trying to form a Two-State solution in Israel. We continue to ask Israel to give up even more land for peace. It is wrong to do so! This land is not ours to divide. This land belongs to God and He wants His people back into the land. God is not pleased with the nations dividing the land. Soon the fulfillment of Joel 3:2 will be seen. All nations will be judged in the valley of Jehoshaphat (The Kedron Valley).

Joel 3:2 *"I will also gather all nations, and bring them down to the Valley of Jehoshaphat; and I will enter into judgment with them there on account of My people, My heritage Israel, whom they have scattered among the nations; they have also divided up My land."*

Oil Diplomacy

In the 1930's, oil was discovered in the Arab countries. Consequently, "oil diplomacy" was instituted. British foreign policy simply bowed to Arabs in an effort of appeasement. In 1939, the British White Paper banned further immigration to Palestine. In addition, with brutal callousness, the United States, and most other nations refused to accept into their countries the beleaguered Jews of Europe.

Then, in the 1930's, anti-Semitism reared its ugly head in Germany in the form of the Nazi party and its leader Adolph Hitler, who found an easy scapegoat for German economic conditions in its Jewish population. As Europe was in World War II by the expansionist attacks of the German blitzkrieg, Hitler, and his henchmen escalated their overt anti-Semitism, proposing a "final solution" to the "Jewish problem", nothing less than a mass extermination of Jewish men, women, and children that if successful would have resulted in genocide.

Thus began the *Shoah* (Hebrew word for holocaust). Systematically and unrelentingly, Jews were arrested throughout Europe, wherever the Third Reich gained ascendancy. First, they were executed and buried in mass graves. Later, a more efficient killing system was devised. Jews were herded into railroad cattle cars and transported to specially prepared death camps, where they were brought into gas chambers. Under the guise of being given showers, lethal cyanide gas was introduced, killing all the occupants. Then, after their corpses had been desecrated, removing anything of value, including in some cases even their skin, they were reduced to ashes in the crematoria that sent up the smoke of the holocaust in which six million Jews were killed, including more than one million children.

When the war concluded and the Allied forces discovered the full nature of history's greatest concentrated atrocity against any people group, the corporate conscience of the world was pricked by the plight of the Jews. Part of this guilt resulted from the fact that the Allied nations shared complicity in the slaughter of the Jews by not allowing early Jewish immigration into their nations and then by not intervening when they had gained knowledge of the concentration camps and the systematic slaughter that was carried out there.

Finally, on May 14, 1948, the United Nations recognized the Jewish people's right to self-determination in establishing their own state in the land of their ancestors. Thus was the nation of Israel restored after nearly 2000 years of nonexistence. Its formation and recognition by the United Nations was a miracle; however, its survival in its earliest years was a greater miracle as Israeli patriots defended the nation despite being vastly outnumbered.

The rebirth of Israel as a nation in 1948 is a literal fulfillment of Ezekiel 37 with the picture of the valley of dry bones. God said to Ezekiel, "Can these bones live?" Ezekiel answers, "LORD, only You know!" Though they were scattered, and though they had lost hope, God brings them together again. They become a mighty army!

They even had their ancient language restored! Eliezer ben Yehudah formulated a Hebrew dictionary around 1909 and the language was restored! Today Jewish people everywhere speak Hebrew.

The Creation Of The Flag Of Israel

In October of 1948, the Provisional Council of the State of Israel adopted the blue and white colors with the Shield of David as the flag of Israel.

The Provisional Council of State
Proclamation of the Flag of the State of Israel

The Provisional Council of State hereby proclaims that the flag of the State of Israel shall be as illustrated and described below: The flag is 220 cm. long and 160 cm. wide. The background is white and on it are two stripes of dark sky-blue, 25 cm. broad, over the whole length of the flag, at a distance of 15 cm. from the top and from the bottom of the flag. In the middle of the white background, between the two blue stripes and at equal distance from each stripe is a Star of David, composed of six dark sky-blue stripes, 5.5 cm. broad, which form two equilateral triangles, the bases of which are parallel to the two horizontal stripes.

25 Tishrei 5709 (28 October 1948)

Provisional Council of State

Joseph Sprinzak, Speaker

This flag was subsequently unfurled on May 11, 1949, at Lake Success in New York when Israel became the fifty-ninth member of the United Nations. That flag has flown over the nation for almost seventy years now, a testimony to the sovereignty and faithfulness of God in bringing to pass his prophetic promises to His chosen people.

The first person to voice the idea that blue and white should be the colors of the Jewish people was an Austrian poet named Ludwig August Frankl (1810-1894). In 1864, he expressed his idea in a poem titled, "Judah's Colors"

> *"When sublime feelings his heart fill,*
> *He is mantled in the colors of his country.*
> *He stands in prayer, wrapped*
> *In a sparkling robe of white.*
>
> *The hems of the white robe*
> *Are crowned with broad stripes of blue;*
> *Like the robe of the High Priest*
> *Adorned with bands of blue threads.*
>
> *These are the colors of the beloved country.*
> *Blue and white are the borders of Judah.*
> *White is the radiance of the priesthood,*
> *And blue, the splendors of the firmament."*

Zionist tradition credits the design of the Zionist flag to David Wolffsohn. During a meeting in Basel, Herzl raised the question of the Zionist flag. Herzl's proposal of a white flag with seven gold stars was not gaining support. Wolffsohn stood up and said, "Why do we have to search? Here is our national flag." Upon which he displayed his prayer shawl and showed everyone the national flag: a white field with blue stripes along the margin.

The design of the Israeli flag is the same as that of the Zionist flag which was used at the First Zionist Congress in Basel, Switzerland, in 1897. David Wolfsohn succeeded Theodor Herzl as president of the World Zionist Organization in 1905. This is Wolfsohn's own written account of the development of the Zionist flag which became the Israeli flag:

"At the behest of our leader Herzl, I came to Basel to make preparations for the Zionist congress, to assure its success and to avoid any opening for detractors. Among the many problems that occupied me then was one which contained something of the essence of the Jewish problem. What flag would we hang in the Congress Hall? Then an idea struck me. We have a flag – and it is blue and white. The tallit which we wrap ourselves when we pray: that is our symbol. Let us take this tallit from its bag and unroll it before the eyes of Israel and the eyes of all nations. So, I ordered a blue and white flag with the Shield of David painted on it. That is how our national flag that flew over Congress Hall came into being. And, no one expressed any surprise or asked whence it came, or how."

It doubtless was a stroke of divine providence that the nation which God originally chose to be a kingdom of priests should, in its restoration, be represented by a flag patterned after the tallit. God predicted that the temple of His people would be a "house of prayer for all people". Israel is to be a praying nation. It is altogether appropriate, then, that the symbol of this nation should be patterned after the prayer shawl in which observant Jews wrap themselves for morning prayers.

Just as the individual Jew covers himself in the tallit as a symbol of his being enshrouded in the Torah and thereby in God, so the nation, whether wittingly or not, is covered with the same symbol of blessing and divine protection. Every day that the flag is flown is representative of Israel's trust in the blessing and protection of God over their nation. When they see the blue, they are reminded of the commandments of God as well as their status a king and priest to God. The blue takes their thoughts back to Moses, who is their spiritual leader concerning the law. The star of David brings to mind their military leader, King David, who was the first to make Jerusalem the capital city of the Jewish people. It also encourages every Jewish man, woman, and child that the Goliath's of this world are no match for one Israeli who comes in the name of the LORD. The white background of the flag reminds the nation that they are to be holy even as He is holy.

The Israeli flag may well even be a fulfillment of a psalm of King David: "*You have given a banner* (flag) *to those that who fear You, that it may be displayed because of the truth*" (Psalm 60:4). Being patterned after the tallit, it certainly is designed after an object which represents and displays truth (the Torah) to Jews around the world. It also represents God's sovereign action demonstrating his intentions to overshadow his people with his wings. The Jewish flag is given to them by God Himself.

The Hebrew word for a banner, or flag, is נס (transliterated as nes). When a possesive form is used, as in "my banner", the word becomes in Hebrew נסי (tranliterated as nissi).

However "nes" has another meaning as well. It also means "miracle". When Joshua was fighting the Amelekites (Exodus 17:8-16), Aaron and Hur held up Moses' arms. As a result, Joshua won the battle and Moses erected an altar and called it "Yahwey Nissi". Most translations translate this as the LORD my banner. However, when you know of the alternate meaning of the word nissi, it is obvious that this should be "The LORD my Miracle"!

Therefore, the Jewish flag, that flys so proudly over the nation of Israel, is a continuous testimony of the miracle power of God over this nation.

Indeed, God has been the protector of Israel. As soon as Israel declared independence on May 15, 1948, she found herself in an untenable situation. The new state was populated almost entirely by war refugees. In addition, it possessed no means of protection. With no army and no weapons, she was a sitting duck. According to legend, the fledgling nation possessed approximately five machine guns with about fifteen rounds of ammunition and one tank.

The United States Holds Back Support

The Jews won their war of independence with minimal help from the West. In fact, they won despite efforts to undermine their military strength.

Although the United States vigorously supported the partition resolution, the State Department did not want to provide the Jews with the means to defend themselves. "Otherwise," Undersecretary of State Robert Lovett argued, "the Arabs might use arms of U.S. origin against Jews, or Jews might use them against Arabs." Consequently, on December 5, 1947, the U.S. imposed an arms embargo on the entire region.

Many in the State Department, however, saw the embargo as yet another means of hindering partition. President Truman nevertheless went along with it hoping it would be a means of averting bloodshed. This was naive given Britain's rejection to suspend weapons shipments to the Arabs and subsequent agreements to provide additional arms to Iraq and Transjordan.

The Arabs had no difficulty obtaining all the arms they needed. In fact, Jordan's Arab Legion was armed and trained by the British, and led by a British officer. At the end of 1948 and beginning of 1949, British RAF planes flew with Egyptian squadrons over the Israel-Egypt border. On January 7, 1949, Israeli planes shot down four of the British aircraft.

The Jews, on the other hand, were forced to smuggle weapons, principally from Czechoslovakia. When Israel declared its independence in May 1948, the army did not have a single cannon or a tank. Its air force consisted of nine obsolete planes. Although the Jewish army had 60,000 trained fighters, only 18,900 were fully mobilized, armed and prepared for war. On the eve of the war, chief of operations Yigael Yadin told David Ben-Gurion: "The best we can tell you is that we have a 50/50 chance."

51

The armies of seven Arab nations (Egypt, Jordan, Syria, Lebanon, Iraq, Arabia, and Yemen) boasted that they would "push the Jews into the sea." Outnumbered 100 to 1, Israel not only repelled the invaders but also acquired more of Palestine than was granted in the UN partition plan. Yigael Yadin, Israel's commander of operations in that war had an amazing explanation of Israel's victory. "It was a Miracle!"

As if to give Israel a false sense of hope, the surrounding Arab nations did not attack immediately. They planned a major offensive against Israel for the eighth day after the declaration of statehood. However, the Israelis, understanding that their very lives were yet again on the line, came up with a plan that they hoped would at least buy them some time to prepare for war. On May 23rd, at midnight, they lined up cars, trucks, taxis, and anything they could find with an engine, side by side along the beaches from Tel Aviv through Netanya and Haifa. They then removed the exhaust pipes from the vehicles, making them sound much louder.

They then loaded large oil drums with rocks and took them to the top of the adjacent hill. When the time was right, early in the morning, the signal was given and the engines were started while the oil drums were rolled down the hill.

The unsuspecting Arab forces were suddenly awakened by the incredible noise, which completely shook the area. Since they had no idea of where the racket was coming, they could only guess – and they assumed that American forces had come to Israel's rescue with Sherman Tanks.

The entire Arab army fled, leaving behind a treasure trove of artillery and thus arming the Israelis.

The victory of the 1948 war was a big miracle composed of a series of little miracles. Over 2500 years ago, the Prophet Isaiah made a remarkable prophecy regarding Israel re-gathering back in the land. Isaiah 41:12 – 13

"You shall seek them and not find them, those who contended with you. Those who war against you shall be as nothing, as a nonexistent thing.

52

For I, the LORD your God, will hold your right hand, saying to you, "Fear not, I will help you'."

More examples of Miracles during Israel's war of independence

A Syrian column of 200 armored vehicles – including 45 tanks attacked Degania, the oldest Kibbutz in Israel. Without artillery, Jewish forces were helpless to block the Syrian advance. There were only 4 heavy weapons (howitzers), the type the French army used in the Franco-Prussian war. Two were promptly dismantled, rushed to Degania and Lieutenant Colonel Moshe Dayan (the local commander) had them re-assembled at the precise moment that the first Syrian tanks entered the Kibbutz. With their first shot, they scored a direct hit. The Syrians thought that they were facing batteries of artilleries and fled!

Miracles continued...

Another miracle worth mentioning took place at Safed, where a small unit of Israeli defenders was holding off a 1000 Arabs. When everything seemed hopeless, a "sudden" tropical storm broke loose. The defenders in desperation took their remaining gasoline and poured it over empty drums, set them alight and rolled them down the hill. Together with the tropical storm the rumbling of the hollow barrels striking rocks created such an illusion that the bewildered attackers thought some sort of secret weapon was released and so they fled.

The "wrong turn" miracle

Twenty-four homemade Israeli armored trucks and cars took a wrong turn on the way to aid a besieged Kibbutz. They crossed and accidentally entered Lebanon. They realize their mistake when they ran into twenty brand new Syrian armored cars traveling with dozens of Syrian supply trucks carrying ammunition and artillery. The Israelis immediately fired at the first Syrian truck and amazingly hit a tank loaded with gasoline, causing an explosion, which set fire to the following truck full of hand grenades. One by one, each truck in the

Syrian convoy exploded. The loud booms could be heard for miles and the scared surviving Syrians abandoned their cargo. The Israelis had just enough people to drive the captured armored vehicles and Syrian weapons back. By the time they finally reached the Kibbutz, the Arab besiegers had already left. Apparently, after they heard rumors that the Israeli forces invaded Lebanon, they fled back to Syria. That is how one wrong turn saved an entire Kibbutz and provided much-needed arms and equipment to the Israeli army.

Continuing Miracles in the Land

Mark Twain, who visited Israel in 1867, described it like this "Innocents Abroad":

"We traversed some miles of desolate country whose soil is rich enough but is given wholly to weeds - a silent, mournful, expanse… a desolation is here that not even imagination can grace with the pomp of life and action. We reached Tabor safely… We never saw a human being on the whole route. We pressed on toward the goal of our crusade, renowned Jerusalem. The further we went the hotter the sun got and the more rocky, bare, repulsive, and dreary the landscape became… There was hardly a tree or a shrub anywhere… Even the olive and the cactus, those fast friends of a worthless soil, had almost deserted the country. No landscape exists that is more tiresome to the eye than that which bounds the approaches to Jerusalem… Jerusalem is mournful, dreary and lifeless. I would not desire to live here. It is a hopeless, dreary, heartbroken land… Palestine sits in sackcloth and ashes."

From Mark Twain's account, we can sense a sadness that just as the Jewish people was mourning the loss of their land, so the land was mourning their absence. It was almost as though the land was cursed until the return of the Jews!

Reclaiming Wastelands

Ezekiel 36:34 - 36 *"And the wasteland shall be tilled, instead of being a ruin before all passing by. And they shall say this land that was wasted has become like the Garden of Eden. And the wasted, deserted and ruined cities now are fortified and inhabited. And the nations that are left all around you shall know that I, Jehovah, build the ruined places and plant that which was wasted. I, Jehovah, have spoken it, and I will do it."*

Amos 9:14-15 *"I will bring back the captives of My people Israel; they shall build the waste cities and inhabit them; they shall plant vineyards and drink wine from them; they shall also make gardens and eat fruit from them. I will plant them in their land, and no longer shall they be pulled up from the land I have given them," Says the LORD your God."*

It was long assumed that Israel (Palestine) was a wasteland and irreclaimable for agriculture. However, the remains of seventy ancient settlement sites, in one 65 mile stretch of the Jordan Valley alone, bring back to mind what Lot saw in Genesis 13:10. He saw all the plain of Jordan, that it was well-watered, even as the Garden of Eden.

Genesis 13:10 *"And Lot lifted his eyes and saw all the plain of Jordan, that it was well watered everywhere (before the LORD destroyed Sodom and Gomorrah) like the garden of the LORD, like the land of Egypt as you go toward Zoar."*

The Bible and the planting of trees

One of the necessities in the arid country of Israel is re-forestation. The Bible helped them decide what kind of trees to plant. The Bible even showed them where to plant them! Knowing that it is advantageous to plant trees where they had flourished before, they searched the Scriptures to find what kind of trees grew where. They found the answers in the Book of Joshua and in the book of Genesis.

"The first tree that Abraham put in the soil of Beer Sheba was a tamarisk," said Dr. Joseph Weitz, an outstanding authority on reforestation. "Following Abraham's lead, we put out 2,000,000 in the same area. Abraham was right! The tamarisk is one of the few trees that we have found that thrives in the South where yearly rainfall is less than 6 inches."

55

The Bible made Israel an agricultural giant

In Bible times, there were two important rainy seasons in Israel. These are referred to as "the early and the latter rain." However, for many centuries, the "early rain" has been minimal while the "latter rain" and dew have disappeared completely. Since 1978, the "latter rain" is falling again. The precipitation of both has spiraled over the decades, just as predicted in Joel 2:23 – 24. *"Be glad then, you children of Zion,*
And rejoice in the LORD your God; for He has given you the former rain faithfully, and He will cause the rain to come down for you – the former rain, and the latter rain in the first month. The threshing floors shall be full of wheat,
And the vats shall overflow with new wine and oil."

The Bible helped build Israel...

David Ben Gurion, Israel's dynamic first Prime Minister, was an ardent student of the Bible as an accurate history of Israel and its land. He dispatched engineers, horticulturalists, botanists etc., with the Bible in one hand and research tools in the other, and miracles happened.

Following Bible clues, copper and iron mines were established. An engineer stated; "we came upon the slag and furnaces of ancient Israel. We often get the feeling that someone has just left."

Deuteronomy 8:7 - 9 was often framed on the walls of mining offices.

"For the LORD your God is bringing you into a good land, a land of brooks of water, of fountains and springs, that flow out of valleys and hills; a land of wheat and barley, of vines and fig trees and pomegranates, a land of olive oil and honey; a land in which you will eat bread without scarcity, in which you will lack nothing; a land whose stones are iron and out of whose hills you can dig copper."

There are remains of copper mines in the Timna Valley, located in southwestern Arava, some 30 km. north of the Gulf of Eilat. The existence of the remains of copper production at Timna was known from surveys conducted at the end of last century, but scientific attention and public interest was aroused when in the 1930s Nelson Glueck attributed the copper mining at Timna to King Solomon (10th century BCE) and named the site "King Solomon's Mines".

The miracle of technology

Israel has witnessed an explosion in both high-tech developments and the number of contracts of Israeli high-tech companies that have been signed with manufacturers all over the world.

Prime Minister Netanyahu said, "We now have the highest per capita of Scientists in the world, this has put Israel on the cutting edge of technology." The New York Stock Exchange lists more high-tech companies from Israel than any other nation.

The miracle of Immigration

Isaiah 43:5 – 6 *"Fear not, for I am with you; I will bring your descendants from the east, and gather you from the west; I will say to the north, "Give them up!" and to the south, "Do not keep them back!" Bring My sons from afar, and My daughters from the ends of the earth".*

Israel's Declaration of Independence stated that Israel will be open for all Jews from all countries of their dispersion to come home. Jewish people kept pouring into Israel ever since independence and is still doing so up to today, increasing the population yearly. The small land of Israel has miraculously increased! On the eve of the 68th anniversary (2016) of its founding, the population of Israel stands at 8,556,000 - 75 percent of it Jewish - up from 7,282,000 since 2008 (Central Bureau of Statistics). The population is continuing to grow at about 1.8% per year.

The Refugee Problem

When the six Arab nations invaded Israel at Israel's birth, many claim 600,000 Arabs were displaced during that war. What is not well known is that approximately 800,000 Jews, who were living in those six Arab nations, had to flee for their lives because of Arab hatred. The solution to this refugee problem would have been simple — a fair exchange.

Israel, at a terrible economic cost, absorbed the 800,000 Jewish refugees. But the Arab nations refused to accept the 600,000 Arab refugees, their Arab brethren. Rather, they placed them in refugee camps, which became dark holes of hate and misery. These were used for propaganda, to turn world opinion against Israel. They succeeded.

Had the Arab countries any true intentions of helping their beleaguered brethren from western Palestine, they would and could have absorbed them easily 4 decades ago, as the Israelites did of an even greater number of Jewish refugees from Arab lands. The Palestinian Arabs share the same language, religion and culture, and for 70% of them, the same countries of origin. Just 3 generations before their grandfathers immigrated, for economic reasons, to Palestine from surrounding Arab lands. However, the 22 Arab countries, uninterested in aiding their Palestinian brothers, preferred to use them as a political weapon to wield against Israel, and the U.N. supported this heartless human manipulation.

In the mid-1970's, Israel attempted to give the Palestinian Arab refugees in Gaza new and better housing. The U.N. General Assembly, at the urging of the Arab states, passed a resolution condemning Israel for trying to relocate these refugees and demanded they be returned "to the camps in which they were removed." And yet, a senior U.N. official came to Gaza in January 1988 accompanied by 10 TV crews on a fact-finding visit and laid the entire blame for the situation at Israel's feet. As if the U.N.'s own complicity in the matter didn't exist!

The God of Israel is a God of miracles --- and He has only begun His miracles in achieving Israel's ultimate destiny. His intentions are revealed by the Prophet Jeremiah.

58

Jeremiah 31:10 *"Hear the word of the LORD, O nations, and declare it in the isles afar off, and say, "He who scattered Israel will gather him, and keep him as a shepherd does his flock."*

The Arab war to destroy Israel failed. Indeed, because of their aggression, the Arabs wound up with less territory than they would have received if they had accepted partition.

The cost to Israel, however, was enormous. Many of its most productive fields lay gutted and mined. Its citrus groves, for decades the basis of the Jewish economy, were largely destroyed. Military expenditures totaled approximately $500 million. Worse yet, 6,373 Israelis were killed, nearly one percent of the Jewish population of 650,000.

Had the West enforced the partition resolution, or given the Jewish people the capacity to defend themselves, many lives might have been saved.

Israel's longest war lasted 1 year 3 months and 10 days starting November 30, 1947. The Arab countries signed armistice agreements with Israel in 1949, starting with Egypt (Feb. 24), followed by Lebanon (March 23), Jordan (April 3) and Syria (July 20). Iraq was the only country that did not sign an agreement with Israel, choosing instead to withdraw its troops and hand over its sector to Jordan's Arab Legion.

God bless you as you continue to stand with Israel. Every year, every day, every minute and every second is a miracle of Israel's existence! The Jewish prayer shawl, in the form of a flag, waves proudly over this land proclaiming that Israel is under the shadow of His wings. This flag seems to be saying to the whole world:

"Pray for the peace of Jerusalem: "May they prosper who love you. Peace be within your walls, prosperity within your palaces." Psalms 122:6-7.

Chapter 4

The Garment of God

(The Shekinah)

Psalm 104:1-2 *"Bless the LORD, O my soul! O LORD my God, You are very great: You are clothed with honor and majesty, who cover Yourself with light as with a garment, who stretch out the heavens like a curtain.*

This Scripture is quoted by one who is putting on the prayer shawl after they have prayed the blessing. In the Jewish mind, it is understood that they are imitating God who clothes Himself with light as with a garment when they are putting on the Prayer Shawl. They are entering into the Light with God.

It is not difficult to imagine God taking a garment and wrapping Himself in it just as an individual would wrap a tallit around himself. So, God wears a tallit. This tallit is made of the material of light. It has to be an immense garment in order to cover the shoulders of an infinite God! Where and how this garment came to be is revealed in the first few verses of the Bible.

In the beginning of God's creation, He spoke two words יהי אור (Yahi Or, pronounced Yah–Hee' Oar). In Hebrew, the verb precedes the noun. Contrary to Western thought, Hebrew places more emphasis on the action than the subject. If we translated these two Hebrew words literally, we would say something like "become light". However, in English we put the subject before the verb so we understand these words as "light be".

What this "light" was is somewhat of a mystery. We know that light must have existed prior to creation because Lucifer name means "light bearer" Lucifer and all the other angels were created long before Genesis the first chapter. So what was this "light"?

In addition, what is the purpose of the creation of the sun and moon if there is already a source of light? Indeed, why would God need light at all? He could easily have created everything in the dark and then put a sun in place for the benefit of man. This creates quite a conundrum.

I believe that the verse in the Bible that began this chapter gives us some understanding into this light. But first let us examine "light" a little further.

When the Israelites were coming out of Egypt God led them with a fire by night and a cloud by day. This has been identified by multiple Jewish sources as "The Shekinah". When the Egyptian army tried to overtake the Israelites, God moved the cloud behind the Israelis. That cloud became darkness on the side of the Egyptians and light on the side of the Israelis. This is similar to what is described in the first day of creation when God "divided" the light from the darkness. The sun and moon were not yet created. Time exists outside of the influences of our sun and moon. Time is in God's hands, not nature's. God established time with the dividing of the light from darkness. God is the author of time.

It easy to see that this "light" in the beginning must have been something similar to what those Israelites experienced coming out of Egypt. When you couple the verse in Psalm 104 where He wraps Himself with light as with a garment, we have the basis for a wonderful teaching concerning Shekinah.

A synonym for Shekinah is Glory. In Isaiah 6:3 it says that the whole earth is full of His Glory! The word "Glory" in Hebrew is כּוֹד (Kabod, pronounced Kah' – Bahd). Therefore, we can see that the Shekinah that was in the beginning with creation is always present even today. The whole earth is full of His Shekinah (Glory).

If that is true, then why do we not see His Glory all around us? I might answer that question with the following analogy.

Right now there are radio waves as well as television signals floating around you. No matter where you go you will have these radio waves and television signals. Even though they are there, you do not hear or see the sounds or the pictures. The reason you do not is because you need to be able to "tune in" to the frequency. In addition, you need the proper equipment to turn that frequency into sound and/or pictures. In much the same way, we need to "tune in" to the Glory.

Another reason we may not be noticing the Glory of the Lord is because we may not know what Glory is. If we do not know what Glory is then we would never know how to recognize it. We speak of the "Glory cloud" and that is certainly one way the Glory is manifest. However, that is not the only way.

When Moses was tending sheep for his father-in-law Jethro he encountered God's Glory. There out of a burning bush God spoke to him.

Then we have Isaiah's description of "the Lord high and lifted up and His train filled the temple". Here the Glory is referred to as a train of a garment. In fact, Jewish sources connect this "train" to the curtain that separated the Holy Place from the Holy of Holies. They call that curtain "The Hem of His garment". This is the same veil (curtain) that was rent from top to bottom at Yeshua's death on the cross.

The Angels at the birth of Yeshua had the Glory of the Lord shining all around them. The shepherds saw the Glory and heard the singing. They then went to see the baby Yeshua.

There are numerous other accounts of the Glory being revealed. Already we have Glory manifested as fire (in a bush), the train of a garment, light shining around angels, and even a cloud leading the children of Israel.

But while all these are physical representations of the Glory of God, they are not really the substance of the Glory. In fact, Moses realized that himself. After seeing the burning bush and seeing the cloud by day and the pillar of fire by night, he wanted more. He realized that the bush and the cloud were just vehicles for the real glory. Moses asked God, "Show me your Glory." (Exodus 33:18)

God granted Moses his request and put him in a cleft of a rock and covered him with His hand. He then passed by him and Moses saw the backside of God. In Exodus 34:5-8 we have the encounter with God's revelation of His Glory to Moses.

"Now the LORD *descended in the cloud and stood with him there, and proclaimed the name of the* LORD. *And the* LORD *passed before him and proclaimed, "The* LORD, *the* LORD *God, merciful* (this should have been translated Compassionate) *and gracious, longsuffering, and abounding in goodness and truth, keeping mercy for thousands, forgiving iniquity and transgression and sin, by no means clearing the guilty, visiting the iniquity of the fathers upon the children and the children's children to the third and the fourth generation."*

So Moses made haste and bowed his head toward the earth, and worshiped. Then he said, "If now I have found grace in Your sight, O Lord, let my Lord, I pray, go among us, even though we are a stiff-necked people; and pardon our iniquity and our sin, and take us as Your inheritance."

There are ten things that God speaks about Himself as He passed by Moses. These ten things are:

1. Compassion

2. Grace

3. Longsuffering

4. Goodness

5. Truth

6. Mercy (hesed)

7. Forgiving iniquity (the word is depravity)

8. Forgiving transgression

9. Forgiving sin

10. Judgment ("no wise clearing the guilty")

Moses fully understood what God was showing Him. He bows his head in worship. God's glory is not a physical manifestation. God's glory is a spiritual radiance of His character. Moses requested that God go with them because he knew that they would need God to teach them more about His character if they were to ever understand His glory.

Here is the secret to tapping into the Glory of God that is everywhere present. Begin by exhibiting the character and nature of God in everything you say and do. Show compassion, be gracious, extend longsuffering, exhibit goodness, hold on to Truth, show mercy, forgive iniquity, transgression and sin, all the while being just in judgment for those who continue in iniquity, transgression, and sin. By doing so you will be showing the Glory of the Lord. It wouldn't surprise me if you were to see a cloud or a fire or an exceedingly bright light around you. After all, when Moses came down after this encounter, his face shone!

I am aware that it is very hard to do these things. However, I do not believe it is impossible. But the only way to accomplish this is to spend time with Him. By spending time with Him we will "be changed from glory to glory". I can think of no better way of spending time with Him than being surrounded by the prayer shawl.

The prayer shawl reminds you that you are imitating God who clothes Himself with light (glory). You, then, are wrapping the tallit around your shoulders as a symbol of wrapping yourself in his Glory (His character). You are actually "putting on" His character and nature. As you grow in His character and nature, you will glorify God through your good works.

In Psalm 61:4 David says, *"I long to dwell in your tent* (tallit) *forever and take refuge in the shelter of your wings* (tzitzit)". God has a garment, it is His Glory (His character and nature). He desires to clothe you with His garment, His garment of light (which is His Glory and Shekinah).

There are two kinds of garments in Scripture. The first are ones we are to put off. The other are ones we are to put on. Another way of describing these garments is one is man-made and the other is God-made. The man-made garments are to be put off or cast away. The God-made garment is to be put on. They are for us a raiment of glory and holiness and beauty.

In the Garden, after man sinned, he made fig leaves for a garment. God comes along and makes them coats of skin. Man-made garments did not cover, only a God-made garment would cover.

Elijah went into heaven and dropped his mantle down to Elisha (II Kings 2:12-13). The first thing Elisha did was to rend his mantle and pick up Elijah's mantle. Earthly mantles are so much inferior to Heavenly mantles. Man may promote himself, or have others promote him, but the promotion that comes from Heaven is far more important and vital.

One day, Yeshua was passing by. On the side of the road was a poor blind beggar (Mark 10:46-52). When Yeshua called for him, he cast aside his garment and went to Yeshua. He would not need his beggar's garment anymore! He was going to receive his sight! He would soon be able to be self-sufficient.

We have the prodigal son (Luke 15:11-32). When he came home in his rags and dirt and filth, the father said, "Bring the best robe, and put it on him". No longer wallowing around in the pig pen of sin and disobedience, He was a son of a loving Father! Not just any robe, only the best robe.

This speaks of a robe like Joseph's coat of many colors (the special tallit). This meant that he would be placed as the favored son with the rights of the first-born. No wonder the elder brother was so angry!

But wait, do you see what the Father said to the elder son? "Son, you are ever with me. You could have had a feast anytime you wanted. All you had to do was ask. I would have gladly given you the best robe, as well".

How often we miss what we could have had, if we had only asked! Like the elder son, many times we are so busy doing things for the Father, when all the Father wants is for us to be His son. Doing, instead of being; modeling our life after Martha's example of serving and doing, instead of Mary's example of devotion.

Yeshua, in Luke 4:16-21, quotes from Isaiah 61:1-3. *"The Spirit of the Lord GOD is upon Me, because the LORD has anointed Me To preach good tidings to the poor; He has sent Me to heal the brokenhearted, to proclaim liberty to the captives, and the opening of the prison to those who are bound; to proclaim the acceptable year of the LORD, and the day of vengeance of our God; to comfort all who mourn, to console those who mourn in Zion, to give them beauty for ashes, the oil of joy for mourning, the garment of praise for the spirit of heaviness; that they may be called trees of righteousness, the planting of the LORD, that He may be glorified."*

Look at that verse! "To proclaim liberty to the captives and the opening of the prison to them that are bound." Notice what he provides for these captives who are liberated. He gives them new garments! These are God-made garments. They are garments of joy and beauty, praise and life!

Joseph, down in the dungeon and in the prison, when Pharaoh called for him to stand in the presence of the king, it says, "And he changed his raiment" (Gen 41:14). Jehoachin, the king of Israel, when he was carried away in the Babylonian captivity, the Babylonian king liberated him. II Kgs 25:29 says, "And he changed his prison garments; and did eat bread".

When you stand in the presence of the King, you cannot wear the clothes of the old life, dirty clothes, clothes of self-righteousness, pride, egotism, worldliness, a slave of satan, following and panting after him. In Christ, we are liberated. We are out of prison. We stand in the presence of the King, and He gives us new clothes.

What kind of garments are those that God gives us? How do they do? What are they like? How do they last?

70

In Deuteronomy 29:5 we have a description of the garments of the Lord. *"And I have led you forty years in the wilderness: your clothes are not waxen old upon you, and your shoe is not waxen old upon your foot"*. The garments of the Lord will last! He doesn't just give you the garment of praise, He gives you praise that keeps bubbling and bubbling over and over! He gives you the oil of joy that keeps flowing and flowing! He gives you beauty that keeps shining and shining!

Not only do the garments last but you can wear them in the fire! In Daniel 3:20-27 it says that there was not even the smell of fire on their garments! When the fires of this life come on your life, just get into the clothing that God provides. It is His praise, joy and beauty that will carry you through! No matter what you are facing, Yeshua will be there if you have on the proper garment. So many times we forfeit our own deliverance because we take off the God-made garment of joy, praise, and beauty.

Look at Ephesians 6:10-18. This is the garment God gives us for warfare! You have your loins girt about with truth. You have the breastplate of righteousness. You have your feet shod with the preparation of the Gospel of peace. You have the shield of faith, the helmet of salvation, and the Sword of the Spirit, which is the Word of God.

Soon Yeshua will come for us to that final wedding ceremony where we no longer will be betrothed but will be in full marriage to the One we love. Look what the Bible says about that glorious event.

Revelation 19:6-9 *"And I heard, as it were, the voice of a great multitude, as the sound of many waters and as the sound of mighty thunderings, saying, "Alleluia! For the Lord God Omnipotent reigns! Let us be glad and rejoice and give Him glory, for the marriage of the Lamb has come, and His wife has made herself ready." And to her it was granted to be arrayed in fine linen, clean and bright, for the fine linen is the righteous acts of the saints.*

Then he said to me, "Write: "Blessed are those who are called to the marriage supper of the Lamb!" And he said to me, "These are the true sayings of God."

The Bride has made herself ready. Not with those garments of this world and of this life. No! The Bride has made herself ready with fine linen, clean and white; for the fine linen is the righteousness of the saints. Blessed (Happy) are they which are called unto the marriage supper of the Lamb.

I do hope that you have this wedding garment. If not, you may do so right now. He wants to take you out of the prison you are in. He wants to clothe you with His glory, his joy, his beauty. If you will just stop reading right now and pray this prayer.

"Dear Heavenly Father, I know that I am a sinner. I know that I am not living for You right now. I know that I do not have the wedding garment on. I want you to forgive me and cleanse my life at this very moment. I give you my life. I give you my hopes, I give you my dreams. From this day on I intend to follow You, with Your help. I renounce satan and all his lies. I declare that this very day I am breaking all ties with my past. I accept the blood of your son Yeshua over my heart. I am asking that Yeshua come into my heart and begin the work of making me in in His image. I receive the gift of Eternal Life right now. I accept the forgiveness that you have so graciously offered. Thank you for saving me."

If you prayed this prayer in sincerity, then you are now a child of God. You are born again. You have been translated from the kingdom of darkness into His marvelous light. You are a brand new man!

Chapter Five
Under His Wings

Numbers 15:37-41 "*Again the LORD spoke to Moses, saying,* "*Speak to the children of Israel: Tell them to make tassels on the **corners** of their garments throughout their generations, and to put a blue thread in the tassels of the **corners**. And you shall have the tassel, that you may look upon it and remember all the commandments of the LORD, and do them, and that you may not follow the harlotry to which your own heart and your own eyes are inclined, and that you may remember and do all My commandments, and be holy for your God. I am the LORD your God, who brought you out of the land of Egypt, to be your God: I am the LORD your God.*"

Deuteronomy 22:12"*You shall make tassels on the four **corners** of the clothing with which you cover yourself.*"

The word translated "corners" is the Hebrew word "kanaph" (כָּנָף). This is translated throughout the Bible as corner, wing, hem, skirt, and lock (as in hair). In the New Testament and in the Septuagint, the Greek word that is used for the Hebrew word kanaph is kraspedon (κρασπέδον). So, then, when you see the words corner, wing, hem, skirt, or lock in the various Bible translations, you will be able to see within the context whether it is referring to the tzitzit on the corner of the garment.

The translators over the centuries, because of anti-Semitic beliefs, have obfuscated the Jewish references out of the Bible. As a result, it has taken much of the richness and meaning out of the text. I am going to attempt to restore much of what has been lost to the Christian community in the next chapters of this book.

Let us begin by looking at a wonderful Psalm.

Psalms 91 "*He who dwells in the secret place of the Most High shall abide under the shadow of the Almighty. I will say of the Lord, "He is my refuge and my fortress; my God, in Him I will trust." Surely He shall deliver you from the snare of the fowler and from the perilous pestilence. He shall **cover you with His feathers**, and **under His wings** you shall take refuge; His truth shall be your shield and buckler. You shall not be afraid of the terror by night, nor of the arrow that flies by day, or of the pestilence that walks in darkness, nor of the destruction that lays waste at noonday. A thousand may fall at your side, and ten thousand at your right hand; but it shall not come near you. Only with your eyes shall you look, and see the reward of the wicked. Because you have made the Lord, who is my refuge, even the Most*

*High, your dwelling place, no evil shall befall you, nor shall any plague come near your dwelling; **For He shall give His angels charge over you, to keep you in all your ways. In their hands they shall bear you up, lest you dash your foot against a stone.** You shall tread upon the lion and the cobra, the young lion and the serpent you shall trample underfoot. "Because he has set his love upon Me, therefore I will deliver him; I will set him on high, because he has known My name. He shall call upon Me, and I will answer him; I will be with him in trouble; I will deliver him and honor him. With long life I will satisfy him, and show him My salvation."*

The book of Psalms is divided into five separate sub-books. Each of the five sub-books corresponds to the Torah (the five books of Moses).

1. Psalm 1 – 41, corresponds to the book of Bereshith (Genesis), pronounced bare-eh-sheeth'.
2. Psalms 42 – 72, corresponds to the book of Shemot (Exodus), pronounced sheh-moht'.
3. Psalms 73 – 89, corresponds to the book of Vayikra (Leviticus), pronounced vah-ee-krah'.
4. Psalms 90 – 106, corresponds to the book of Bamidbar (Numbers), pronounced bah-meed-bahr'.
5. Psalms 107 – 150, corresponds to the book of Devarim (Deuteronomy), pronounced deh-vah-reem'.

Psalms 91, then, fits within the group of Psalms that corresponds to the book of Bamidbar (Numbers). Bamidbar is Hebrew for "In the wilderness". It is fitting, then, for us to consider this Psalm to be a sort of guide for us through our own "wilderness wanderings".

Like the Israelites of old, who moved around in temporary tents, we also are sojourners in a land that is not our own. The Israelites had not yet come into their promised land. That would be left for the Joshua generation. As the song says, *"This world is not my home. I'm just passing through. My treasures are laid up, somewhere beyond the blue. The angels beckon me from Heaven's golden shore and I can't feel at home in this world anymore."*

While in this world, we need to know how to live victoriously. Psalm 91 gives us the answer, *"He who dwells in the secret place of the*

Most High". This speaks of "dwelling", not "visiting". You cannot live victoriously by "visiting" the secret place.

What is the "secret place" that the Psalmist is speaking? Moses was commanded to build a tabernacle with three sections. First was the Outer Court where the Brazen Altar for sacrifice and the Brass Laver for sanctification were placed. Second came the Holy Place where the Candlestick, the Table of Showbread, and the Altar of Incense were housed. Finally came the Holy of Holies where was placed the Ark of the Covenant with the Mercy Seat sitting as a lid over the Ark. Above the Mercy Seat, there were two Cherubim facing each other with wings outstretched. This is also known as the "secret place".

I want to focus right now on the wings stretched over the Mercy Seat. When the Psalmist is speaking of God covering us with His feathers and that under His wings we will trust, he is not talking about a bird or any other fowl. He is picturing the wings of the Cherubim. He actually sees those who dwell in the secret place as one who is continually at the Mercy Seat being shadowed by the wings of God. He even goes on to say, "He will give His angels charge over you". I believe the Psalmist was picturing the Cherubim as he was writing these very words.

If we are going to understand what the Psalmist is saying about "under His wings you will take refuge", we will need to know what Cherubim are. ("Cherubim" is the plural form of the word Cherub.) Nowhere in the Bible is any Cherub or Cherubim referred to as an angel or angels. This brings us to an interesting conundrum. If Cherubim are not angels, then what are they?

The first time we see Cherubim in the Bible is in the book of Genesis. After man sinned, God placed Cherubim to "guard" the Garden of Eden. While that does not tell us what they are, it does tell us what they do.

Ezekiel has a vision of the Cherubim and he describes them as having four faces. Ezekiel, chapter one states, "*As for the likeness of their faces, each had the face of a man; each of the four had the face of a lion on the right side, each of the four had the face of an ox on the left side, and each of the four had the face of an eagle.*" Each Cherub had four faces, man, lion, ox,

78

and an eagle. Now, we know what they look like, but still do not know what they are.

Ezekiel, chapter ten tells us that the Cherubim are carriers of the Glory of God. He describes, in vivid detail how that the Glory only moved as the Cherubim moved.

Since we are not told in the Scriptures what the Cherubim are, then we will have to be satisfied with only knowing what they look like and what they do. However, that in itself is amazing!

These same four faces appear all through the Bible, from Genesis through Revelation. Every time they appear, we will know that they are guarding something or carrying God's glory.

In Moses Tabernacle, the Cherubim were not only over the Mercy Seat on the Ark of the Covenant, but they were also embroidered into the curtains and on the ceiling of the Tabernacle. As such, they "guarded" and "carried" God's glory.

When Israel was camped around the Tabernacle, four standards (flags or ensigns) stood out higher than the other standards. Judah's standard of the Lion was on the East side. Reuben's standard of a Man was on the South side. Ephraim's standard of an Ox was on the West side. Dan's standard of an Eagle was on the North side. Thus was Israel "guarded" by a representative Cherubim with these four standards.

This "guarding" over Israel was exemplified when Balak hires Balaam to curse Israel in Numbers Chapter 22 through 24. Four times, from four different locations, Balak tried to get Balaam to curse Israel. Every time Balaam ended up blessing Israel. As long as Israel stayed within the boundaries of those four standards they were blessed.

However, Balaam tells Balak how to bring a curse on Israel. In Revelation 2:14 it says, *"But I have a few things against you, because you have there those who hold the doctrine of Balaam, who taught Balak to put a stumbling block before the children of Israel, to eat things sacrificed to idols, and to commit sexual immorality."*

Israel could not be cursed by Balaam, but they could cause a curse to come on themselves by not living within the boundaries of what the standards represent. We will find out what those standards represent shortly.

We see these four faces appear again in Revelation 4:7. They are called the "four beasts". Here they are again "carrying" the glory of God. They cry "Holy, Holy, Holy".

These Cherubim have four wings, or "kanaphs", which is also the Hebrew word for corners. If you remember, the Jewish prayer shawl has four corners. You see, when a Jewish man or woman puts the prayer shawl over their head, they are coming under the wings of the Cherubim and approaching the Mercy Seat to find "grace to help in the time of need". They, then, are entered into the "glory" of God.

Even more than that, they are reminded of the four corners of the earth, N, S, E, and W. This, in turn, reminds them of the four faces. Though they do not realize what these four faces represent and who they are, they are still aware of them.

The four faces each represent a different aspect of the Messiah. Yeshua (Jesus) came as the Lion of the tribe of Judah as presented in Matthew. He came as the Ox (the Servant) as presented in Mark. He came as the Son of Man as presented in Luke. He came as the Eagle (Son of God) as presented in John. The four Gospels were written to reveal the Messiah to the Jewish people through the teaching of the tallit (prayer shawl).

Therefore, unwittingly, when the Jewish man or woman puts on the prayer shawl they are representing that they are being clothed with the Messiah, our Yeshua. Not only that but they are also coming (symbolically) "under His wing". How I earnestly pray they would not only come symbolically but in reality as well!

We may not be told what the Cherubim are, but we can see what they represent. The Cherubim declare to us who Yeshua is. They reflect his glory. It is interesting to note that Lucifer, before his fall, was a Cherub (Ezekiel 28:13). He was the "anointed Cherub that covers (or guards). However, Lucifer wanted the "glory". He no longer wanted to simply "carry" and "guard" the glory. Therein is the admonition for each of us to be careful not to take the glory of that which belongs to God. As the song says, *To God be the glory, great things He has done."*

Let's put this all together. The tallit is a "little tent" that is a personal "Holy of Holies" that one can enter anytime they desire. In this "secret place of the Most High", one comes under the wings of protection. It is but a shadow of a greater truth that is revealed in Christ. Being "in Christ" is a place of protection. Living an "in Christ" life puts us "under His wings". The tallit is representative of being "In Him" and "not of this world". It is a separation from the world and a communion with Him. While living the "in Christ" life you cannot be cursed, you can only be blessed. However, like Israel, if your life does not stay within the boundaries of an "in Christ" life, you will bring a curse upon yourself.

Yeshua wept over Jerusalem and said, "*O Jerusalem, Jerusalem, the one who kills the prophets and stones those who are sent to her! How often I wanted to gather your children together, as a hen gathers her chicks under her wings, but you were not willing!*"

Are you willing to be "under His wings?" Will you live the "in Christ" life? Will you be separated from the world unto Him?

William Cushing in 1896 penned the following hymn titled **Under His Wings:**

Under His wings I am safely abiding,
Though the night deepens and tempests are wild,
Still I can trust Him; I know He will keep me,
He has redeemed me, and I am His child.
Refrain
Under His wings, under His wings,
Who from His love can sever?
Under His wings my soul shall abide,
Safely abide forever.
Under His wings, what a refuge in sorrow!
How the heart yearningly turns to His rest!
Often when earth has no balm for my healing,
There I find comfort, and there I am blessed.
Refrain
Under His wings, oh, what precious enjoyment!
There will I hide till life's trials are o'er;
Sheltered, protected, no evil can harm me,
Resting in Jesus, I'm safe evermore.
Refrain

Chapter Six
The Coat of Distinction

Genesis 37:3-11 *"Now Israel loved Joseph more than all his children, because he was the son of his old age. Also he made him a **tunic of many colors**. But when his brothers saw that their father loved him more than all his brothers, they hated him and could not speak peaceably to him.*

Now Joseph had a dream, and he told it to his brothers; and they hated him even more. So he said to them, "Please hear this dream which I have dreamed: There we were, binding sheaves in the field. Then behold, my sheaf arose and also stood upright; and indeed your sheaves stood all around and bowed down to my sheaf."

And his brothers said to him, "Shall you indeed reign over us? Or shall you indeed have dominion over us?" So they hated him even more for his dreams and for his words.

Then he dreamed still another dream and told it to his brothers, and said, "Look, I have dreamed another dream. And this time, the sun, the moon, and the eleven stars bowed down to me."

So he told it to his father and his brothers; and his father rebuked him and said to him, "What is this dream that you have dreamed? Shall your mother and I and your brothers indeed come to bow down to the earth before you?" And his brothers envied him, but his father kept the matter in mind."

Most people have heard this story in various ways. I want to show you something very profound about this passage of Scripture.

The words "tunic of many colors" is a translation of two Hebrew words (כתנת פסים) that literally translated means "tunic of distinction". We find only one other person who had a garment described by these two Hebrew words. That person was Tamar, the sister of Absalom, who were both children of King David. In II Samuel 13:18 it speaks of a tunic of many colors being the robe of a king's daughter. This means that the robe (coat or tunic) would have had the expensive color of royalty, tekhelet. In addition, it would also have the purple and the scarlet threads. Therefore, we see that Joseph's tunic would have had the blue (tekhelet), purple (argaman), and the scarlet (tola'at shani) and perhaps some other colors.

Joseph's tunic would represent that he was to be the ruler of the family (if his father died). In addition, this garment would mean

86

that Joseph would get the double blessing of his father. No wonder his brothers hated him!

That would have been bad enough, but Joseph dreamed a dream. It was not unusual that Joseph dreamed, nor was the dream all that unusual. After all, in reality, it was only a dream of one day having the respect, honor, and admiration of his peers and his parents.

The only problem, at least for Joseph's brothers, was that Joseph believed his dream! Joseph said that God gave him the dream! Joseph believed his dream was real! Joseph believed his dream was right!

Joseph's brothers had dreams too. Only they put off their dreams as unrealistic, couldn't happen, didn't deserve them, just something for a pie-in-the-sky Pollyanna to believe in. They were too sophisticated to believe in some pipe dream! They knew who they were, and it wasn't any one great!

God gave Joseph a good dream. God does not give bad dreams. He will give you a good dream too. However, He will not tell you what you must go through to have your dream. If he did, you would mess up the process or simply refuse to accept the dream in the first place.

Joseph's dream is prophetic to sustain him through the tough times ahead. I Timothy 1:18 says this, *"This charge I commit to you, son Timothy, according to the prophecies previously made concerning you, that by them you may wage the good warfare"*. Your dream is given so you will have something to hold on to in the circumstances of life.

Joseph had a promise. He believed that promise. Although every circumstance that followed seemed to be the exact opposite of that promise, he believed in the promise. The promise is the sustaining factor in life. The promise gets you over when you should be going under.

Looking up at his brothers from the bottom of the pit, I can hear him say, "One day, it will by you who are looking up to me." As they stripped him of his coat, I can hear him say, "One day you will be stripped and come as beggars to me." As they sold him to the caravan,

I can hear him say, "One day it will be you who will come by caravan and be sold to me."

His promise gave him courage to face adversity and rise above it. Joseph continued to believe his promise. In every circumstance he behaved as if his promise was true. He was the head and not the tail. He was above only and not beneath. Every time he seemingly got knocked down, he rose again!

His promise gave him purpose. His promise gave him purity with Potiphar's wife. His promise gave him patience when the butler took his time to remember him at the palace. His promise gave him promotion, first in Potiphar's house, then in jail, and finally as second in power over all Egypt!

You have a promise! You have a dream! Everyone has a promise. Everyone has a dream. Do you believe in your promise? Do you believe in your dream? You can tell by the way you respond to your circumstances if you believe or not.

Once you choose to believe in your promise, you will have purpose and you will then experience promotion. Purity will become a way of life. Patience for the fulfillment of your dream will be your crowning virtue.

His dream was in direct correlation to the garment that he wore. The garment made Joseph feel important. Rightfully so, his own father gave him this coat. He knew he was loved, he knew he was special. He knew that he had destiny.

Once Joseph shared his dream with his brothers, they hated him even more for his dreams. They hated the idea of him having a dream! They hated what the dream meant! They are in the group of people I call **The Dream Haters**.

When you have a dream, and you believe in that dream, you will always encounter The Dream Haters. They are all around. They will do their best to keep your dream from happening. They will connive, they will plot, they will go as far as to plan your demise, if they can.

On a particular day, Joseph's father sent him to see how his brothers were doing. The brothers could see Joseph, with his tunic of distinction, from a long way off.

It took quite a while for Joseph to get to where his brothers were. When his brothers saw him in the distance, they said, *"Look, this dreamer is coming"*. They then begin to plot his murder! Their hatred had festered in their minds for so long that they were ready to do the unthinkable.

It was because they did not have their father's love that began the feelings of their hatred toward Joseph. Then, the dreams he shared put them in a subservient position, with Joseph ruling over them. If they could just eliminate him, then their father would be free to love them.

If it had not been for Reuben, the brothers would have succeeded in their diabolical desire. Had Joseph been murdered, God's plan for the Seed of Woman would have been forever lost.

Joseph's dream was part of a much larger dream. That dream was God's dream of bringing His Son into the world to free mankind from sin.

Had Joseph died, so would have the entire family of Israel. There would have been no Joseph in Egypt to rise to power in order to save, not only the Egyptians, but also his own family. There would have been no tribe of Judah. There would be no Joseph and Mary. There would have been no Yeshua! There would have been no salvation. You and I would be eternally lost!

You may not realize it now, but your dream is part of a larger dream that may well include blessings upon those that hated your dream in the first place! His brothers meant it for evil, but God meant it for good, to save his family from death.

The Dream Haters will come. You might as well get ready for them. Your attitude toward them will be an important part of the fulfillment of your dreams. Bless them who persecute you. Do good unto them who despitefully use you. By doing this you will show that you are a child of El Elyon, the Most High God (cp. Matthew 5:44 and Luke 6:35)

89

The next group of people who you will encounter when you believe in your dream is **The Dream Takers**. There are at least three types of Dream Takers in this world. The first one is <u>Others Opinion</u>. They will be the ones whose opinions of you matter the most. Your parents, your friends, your colleagues, your spouse, and even your very own self. These are the ones who just can't see you being more than you already are. They can only see you as what you have been, not as what you could be. They see your limitations. They know your weaknesses. They know your failings. They are the ones who are closest to you.

Joseph's parents couldn't believe their ears when Joseph told of his second dream. *"What is this dream that you have dreamed? Shall your mother and I and your brothers indeed come to bow down to the earth before you?"* They knew Joseph. This seemed utterly impossible for them to believe. How could their little boy ever be in such a position as his dream described?

However, the tallit that he wore seemed to validate his dream. So, they *"kept the matter in mind."*

The second type of Dream Taker is <u>Moral Decay</u>. Potiphar's wife tried many times to seduce Joseph. Had Joseph given in, Potiphar would have surely found out. As it was, it is plain that Potiphar did not really believe his wife's accusations. If he had, Joseph would have surely suffered a much worse fate than just being in prison. Again, if Joseph dies, then there is no Savior.

Moral failure will rob you of your God-given dream and destiny. Moral failure will cripple your life. Moral Decay will take your dreams and crumple them in the dirt.

The third type of Dream Taker is <u>Selfish Manipulators</u>. In prison, Joseph rises to the top. Then two men, a butler and a baker, who were also in prison with him have dreams. Joseph interprets both dreams for them. He then asked the butler to remember him when he is restored to his position in the palace. The butler agrees, but later forgets about his promise and about Joseph.

Selfish Manipulators will come and go. They will take advantage of your relationship with the Lord. They will ask you to help them in every way, spiritually, physically and materially. Then, when they are in position to be of aid to you, they will conveniently forget you exist.

It is at this point, that your hopes will seem the farthest from you. You are at your lowest point. Nothing around you remotely looks like the dream you had years before. At the moment you finally have someone who is in position to help you, you put your confidence in them, and they let you down. It is at this point that you will forget your dreams. Your dream will die within you.

But remember this, a dream is a seed. A seed has to die in the ground before it can germinate and break through the hard unyielding soil. Your dream will have to die. It is at this darkest hour that your dream is about to come into reality. It won't look like it, but wait for it anyway. Habakkuk 2:3 *"For the vision is yet for an appointed time; but at the end it will speak, and it will not lie. Though it tarries, wait for it; because it will surely come, it will not tarry."*

The last group of people you will encounter when you believe in your dream are the **Dream Makers**. These are ones who are sent by God to move you along toward the fruition of your dream.

God is the ultimate Dream Maker! All the while Joseph was moving in the direction of his dream, God was there. He was giving Joseph favor in his own father's house, he was giving him favor in Potiphar's house, he was giving him favor in the prison, and he gave him favor in the sight of Pharaoh!

When he finally has the meeting with his brothers in Egypt and he reveals himself to them, he says to them, *"God sent me ahead of you"*. He realized that God was behind the scenes in every one of his circumstances, working for his dream to come to pass.

God is doing the same for you. You may not comprehend it now, but He is working for you. He is busy moving heaven and earth to bring your dream into reality. Talk to Him about your dream. Let Him know that you trust Him with your dream. Let Him know that you know He is making your dream a reality, even if it does not look like it right now.

God has sent a group of individuals into your life, if you will avail yourself of them. They are the equippers, encouragers, enablers, and educators.

One group is the fivefold ministry of the church, Apostles, Prophets, Evangelists, Pastors, and Teachers (Ephesians 4). These are the Dream Makers that God has put in your life to be your helpers. Avail yourself of their ministry to you. By doing so, you will achieve your dream.

There are many other Dream Makers out there. Some are not in the fivefold ministry group. When you find a Dream Maker, then surround yourself with as many as you can. Share your dream with them. Do all you can to help them with their dream, as well. You can never have enough Dream Makers in your life!

We finish this episode with Joseph with the Dream Maker that God gave him. The one who had the most power in all the earth at that time was about to help Joseph achieve his dream. Pharaoh didn't even know that Joseph had a dream, but Pharaoh was the one who enabled Joseph to see his dream come to pass.

Pharaoh has a dream and no one can interpret the dream. The butler tells Pharaoh about Joseph. Joseph interprets the dream and Pharaoh elevates him to 2nd in command of all Egypt! He puts a royal robe on him. Guess what! This robe would have had the tekhelet (blue), purple (argaman), and the scarlet (tola'at shani). Joseph literally gets back his coat of many colors!

Now, I want you to consider something very important. In the beginning, Adam and Eve were created to be co-regents on this earth. They were the king and queen of all creation. They were stripped of that honor through the deception of satan. Nevertheless, Yeshua came and gave us back our dominion. We are kings! We have been given back our tunic of distinction! We now wear a robe of many colors!

In Revelation 1:5b-6 it says:

"...Unto Him that loved us, and washed us from our sins in His own blood, and hath made us kings and priests unto God and His Father; to Him be glory and dominion for ever and ever. Amen."

You have the thread of tekhelet in your blood! You are royalty! You are somebody! You rule and reign in this life! With the exception of God, all things are under your feet! You have authority over all the works of the enemy!

You have a Divine destiny! Go for it! Your dream is real! Your dream is right!

Chapter Seven
Ruth and Boaz

The Prayer Shawl, and in particular the tassels (tzitzit), played an integral part in the engagement and ultimate marriage of Ruth and Boaz. Before we look at the events that led up to the moment that the tzitzit (tassels) become significant, we should introduce the characters that are named in the book of Ruth.

Names are extremely significant in the Bible. Names reveal to us the character of the individual. In this book of the Bible, names reveal to us something very profound. Let us look at the list of names.

- Elimelech means, "My God is king".
- Naomi means, "Pleasant" (she later wanted to be called Marah which means "bitter")
- Mahlon means, "Sickly or Disabled"
- Chilion means, "Pining"
- Bethlehem means, "House of Bread"
- Orpah means, "Stiff-necked"
- Ruth means, "Friend"
- Boaz means, "In Him is Strength"
- Obed means, "Service and Worship"
- Jesse means, "Yahweh Exists"
- David means, "Beloved"

So then the book of Ruth can be told through these names. *"My God is king and Pleasant had two sons named Sickly and Pining. A famine came and they all moved to Moab. The two sons met and married Stiff-necked and Friend. Then, My God is king died. After that Sickly and Pining died. This left Pleasant, Stiff-necked and Friend alone in Moab. Pleasant decides to go back to the House of Bread. Stiff-necked decides to return to the gods of Moab while Friend decided to go to the House of Bread with Pleasant. Through a series of events, Friend meets In Him is Strength. Friend discovers that In Him is Strength is a Kinsman Redeemer and that he is required under the Law of Moses to marry her to raise up an heir for her dead husband Sickly and Disabled. Friend and In Him is Strength have a son by the name of Service and Worship. He then, in turn, has a son by the name of Yahweh Exists. Then Yahweh Exists has a son named Beloved. Beloved becomes God's king in Israel. So we see that My God is King is finally fully realized through Yahweh Exists" son, Beloved (or as we might say Yahweh's Beloved Son.)"*

This is a beautiful synopsis of the book of Ruth. Now let's look deeper into its pages.

To understand the Book of Ruth we have to go back to Genesis. In Genesis 3:15, where we find the first promise in the Bible, there is a promise about the "seed of woman" who would bruise the head of satan. Genesis 49:8-12 tells us that Judah was the tribe from whom Messiah, the seed of woman, would come.

Genesis 49:8-12 *"Judah, you are he whom your brothers shall praise; your hand shall be on the neck of your enemies; your father's children shall bow down before you. Judah is a lion's whelp; from the prey, my son, you have gone up. He bows down, he lies down as a lion; and as a lion, who shall rouse him? The scepter shall not depart from Judah, nor a lawgiver from between his feet, until Shiloh comes; and to Him shall be the obedience of the people. Binding His donkey to the vine, and His donkey's colt to the choice vine, He washed his garments in wine, and His clothes in the blood of grapes. His eyes are darker than wine, and His teeth whiter than milk."*

Back in Genesis 38, we find that Perez is the son of Judah through Tamar. This particular chapter is rich with incredible connections to a number of stories within the Old Testament. Its position seems to be an interruption in the story of Joseph. However, when you understand it, this story offers a contrast between Judah's character and Joseph's character. (While reading this chapter, you must realize that we are dealing with an ancient civilization that does not operate with the same values as we hold today.)

The writer wants us to understand the underlying reason why Joseph had to go to Egypt and then why the Israelites needed to be in bondage. Had these events not happened, the family would have scattered across the area, married pagan wives, and eventually would have lost the "seed of woman". In order to keep the family intact and grow them into a nation of several million people, God would have to take them to Egypt.

The "seed of woman" had come from Abraham to Isaac, then to Jacob. Jacob's oldest son, Reuben, lost his birthright because he slept with Bilhah, his father's concubine (Genesis 35:21-22). Simeon and Levi would have been the next in line, but they had lost their birthright when they had disregarded their father's authority and took matters into their own hands concerning the rape of their sister Dinah (Genesis 34).

This leaves the birthright, as well as the "seed of woman", with Judah the fourth born male. Apparently, Judah takes his new position and lets it go to his head. He moves away from the family business and sets up a business of his own in Canaan, about 30 miles away. He meets and marries a Canaanite woman who subsequently has 3 sons, Er, Onan, and Shelah.

Up until now, it was the father who would direct the marriage of his son to one from his own people. Abraham had got a wife for Isaac with the help of Eliezar. Isaac had sent Jacob back to Padan-Aram to find a wife. Now Judah seeks a wife, all on his own, from a pagan culture.

Problems come immediately. These three boys were no sterling characters! It is said that Er was evil and God slew him. We don't know what evil Er did, but it gives us an insight into the progressive nature of rebellion. Judah had been complicit in Joseph's sale to the caravan as well as the lie told to his father. Now his firstborn son is categorized as "evil". When you sow the wind, you reap the whirlwind.

This provides for us the first mention of what has become known, by the Latin term, the "Levirate law". This means that the nearest relative, usually a brother, would be responsible to have sexual relations with his dead brother's wife in order to raise up an heir (a seed) for him. The son born to this union would receive the double portion birthright blessing from the father.

This was, in effect, a way to provide for the wife of the deceased. It was a protective law that was beneficial to the wife of the deceased and offered nothing for the brother of the deceased. Therefore, we see that the males usually did not respond well to this law.

After Er dies, Judah tells his son Onan to provide an heir for Er's wife. This puts Onan in an unfavorable position. Remember that Onan's mother is a pagan Canaanite. I am sure that he does not care about the "seed of woman". Onan is only concerned about his own inheritance. If Er's wife does not have a male child, then Onan would receive the double portion from Judah. Therefore, even though he does have sexual intercourse with Er's wife, he spills his seed on the ground. This denies Er of an heir. It is a violation of the Levirate law! Consequently, God slays Onan.

There is only one son left, but he is too young to be married. By now Judah sees how corrupt his boys are and that they will not ever accept the God of Abraham. They are too tied to the gods of their mother, the Canaanite. Judah realizes that even if he gives Shelah to Tamar, then God will slay him as well, because it is obvious that his sons are obstinate and rebellious.

Judah tells Tamar to wait until Shelah is grown, but all the while Judah has no intention of having Shelah marry Tamar. Once Tamar realizes this, she decides to take matters into her own hands.

Tamar poses as a prostitute and Judah ends up going to bed with her. Tamar becomes pregnant with twins. When the twin boys are born, the first one's hand comes out and the midwife ties a scarlet thread around the hand. Then the hand goes back and the other boy comes out first. They name him Perez, which means "breach" or "breakthrough", because he breaks through and passes around the firstborn.

The one with the scarlet thread is named Zerah. The meaning of the name Zerah is "rising light", or "dawning". Zerah is the great-grandfather of Achan who took the Babylonian garment from the city of Jericho in Joshua's day.

The younger, Perez, is chosen over the older, Zerah. The promise of the "Seed" is now in Perez. This is last we see of this seed; it goes unrevealed in Exodus through Judges. We do not hear anything about the "seed of woman".

Seemingly, the Bible leaves us pondering the hope of this Seed line until a young lad, by the name of David, appears from Bethlehem of Judah (I Samuel 17:12). He is anointed as king by Samuel and then promised a continuation of his seed on the throne of Israel in II Samuel 7 (the Davidic Covenant). As the king, the Seed of the Woman is perpetuated in David.

But where is the Seed from Exodus to I Samuel? The book of Ruth is the connection we are looking for. It is for this very reason that the book of Ruth is in the Bible.

The book of Ruth introduces us to an individual family. What makes this family important? There is the head of the family, Elimelech. Why is he important?

The first name we encounter and the last name we read about tells us the purpose of the book of Ruth. Elimelech (My God is King) begins the narrative and then ends with David (the King chosen by God). It is a story of how Israel goes from God being King over the nation to having an earthly king who is chosen by God. It is the bridge between these two events.

The book of Ruth is obviously written after David became king of Israel. This book is vital is demonstrating that King David was the one who was to begin God's choice of kings until the King of kings came to set up His throne. It is King David who is the link between the prophecy over Judah and its fulfillment in King Messiah. It is important because King Saul was not God's choice, however, King David was His choice. So the purpose of this story is to show how King David became the one who would be in the line for the coming Messiah.

Therefore, the book of Ruth is revealing to us a connection to the genealogy of the coming King (the seed of woman of Genesis 3:15). In fact, the mention of the term "Bethlehem-Judah" is meant to stir up questions in the reader's mind. The use of the word "Judah" is to direct us back to Genesis 39 where Judah is identified as the tribe from where Messiah would come. This would then naturally bring us to Perez, the son of Judah. It also connects the events where Ruth and Boaz are ultimately united to the events surrounding Perez's conception in Genesis 38. We will see the correlation as we continue with the narrative of Ruth.

The book starts with the times of the Judges and a relatively unidentified man named Elimelech. It ends with "David", the Old Testament "Seed of Woman" who prefigured the coming of the King Messiah. So, whoever Elimelech is, he will begin a story which will lead to the Seed of Woman. It begins with an unknown individual man in Israel and ends with the hope of the Messiah in David, the King.

To understand who Elimelech is we need to start where the story ends. The ending is "David". But who was David's father? His father was Jesse. Who was Jesse's father? His father was Obed. Who was Obed's father? His father was Boaz. Boaz is Ruth's husband.

Now, that may be all most of the readers of the book of Ruth are interested in because we now have a tie back to Ruth in the story. But that is not where this line stops in tracing Messiah's seed. It goes back further. Boaz' father was Salmon (husband of Rahab the harlot of Jericho fame). Salmon's father was Nahson. Nahson's father was Aminadab. Aminadab's father was Aram. Aram's father was Hezron. Hezron's father was Perez. The father of Perez was Judah (Matthew 1:3-6). This is where we left off with the "Seed of woman" in Genesis.

Now we know that Boaz and Ruth are linked to the "seed of woman" through genealogy, but where does Elimelech fit in? After all, he is the first name mentioned.

Boaz was not first in line to be the patriarch of the Seed. The "nearer kinsman" was before Boaz, meaning he was Boaz's elder brother. The Levirate law of Deuteronomy 25:5-10 says that if a man dies without a child, then that man's brother would then take the dead man's wife and produce a child in his dead brother's name.

Elimelech had died and his two sons also died. This made it possible for a "near kinsman" to marry the wife of Elimelech and produce a child through Naomi. But Naomi is too old to have children and so Naomi hatches a plan to have Boaz, a "near kinsman", marry Ruth, the wife of Elimelech's son Mahlon who also is dead.

Therefore, it is seen that Boaz had at least two older brothers, the "nearer kinsman" and Elimelech. An abbreviated genealogy would look like this:

Judah
Perez
Salmon
Elimelech   Near Kinsman   Boaz
Mahlon   Chilion

Therefore, we begin the book of Ruth with Elimelech because he is the beginning of the link of the seed of the woman that we left with Perez in Genesis.

So now that Elimelech has been tied to the one who has the Seed of the Woman, what happens to him? Elimelech has two sons. The oldest is Mahlon. Elimelech dies. So, Mahlon has the Seed line. Then Mahlon dies. Normally it would pass to the next oldest, who would be Chilion, but Chilion dies as well.

What happens to the seed now? It goes back to the nearest family blood relative, Elimelech's next younger brother, the "nearer kinsman". He now has the Seed in him. And he is in Bethlehem.

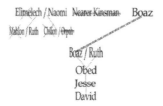

The story starts with Elimelech's family living in Bethlehem. The opening sentence says that this takes place during the times of the Judges. By just turning back one page in your Bible, you will discover the condition of Israel during this time.

Judges 21:25 *"In those days there was no king in Israel: every man did that which was right in his own eyes."*

This is not only the condition of Israel, but it is also the condition of Elimelech (אֱלִימֶלֶךְ) (pronounced El-ee-mel'-ek) and Naomi (נָעֳמִי) (pronounced Nigh'-mee). We are told that there was a famine and that Elimelech and Naomi decided to go to Moab with their two sons Mahlon (מַחְלוֹן) (pronounced Mahk'-lon) and Chilion (כִּלְיוֹן) (pronounced Kil'-ee-on). This was in direct disobedience to God's covenant obligation.

Deuteronomy 7:2-4 *"You shall make no covenant with them nor show mercy to them nor shall you make marriages with them. You shall not give your daughter to their son, nor take their daughter for your son. For they will turn your sons away from following Me, to serve other gods; so the anger of the LORD will be aroused against you and destroy you suddenly."*

Deuteronomy 23:3-6 *"An Ammonite or Moabite shall not enter the assembly of the LORD; even to the tenth generation none of his descendants shall enter the assembly of The LORD forever, because they did not meet you with bread and water on the road when you came out of Egypt, and because they hired against you Balaam the son of Beor from Pethor of Mesopotamia, to curse you. Nevertheless, The LORD your God would not listen to Balaam, but the LORD your God turned the curse into a blessing for you, because the LORD your God loves you. You shall not seek their peace nor their prosperity all your days forever.*

So this disobedient "doing what is right in their own eyes" family left Bethlehem (the House of Bread) because there was no bread in the House of Bread. Already we are seeing a connection concerning obedience and disobedience.

Disobedience during the time of the Judges had caused a famine. But instead of repenting, Elimelech and Naomi decided to move their family to Moab. This eventually led to the death of Elimelech and his removal from the lineage of the Messiah.

Then the sons Mahlon and Chilion rebelled even further by marrying Moabite women. This disobedience resulted in their deaths and their removal from the lineage of Messiah. James 1:15 says, *"… sin, when it is full grown, brings forth death"*. Also, Ezekiel 18:20 says, *"The soul who sins shall die"*.

This leaves us with Naomi, Ruth, and Orpah alone in Moab. Naomi hears that there was now bread in the House of Bread (Ruth 1:6). Ruth and Orpah should be able to find suitable husbands in Moab. However, Ruth and Orpah decide to follow Ruth back to Bethlehem, where neither of them had any hopes of finding a husband. No Jewish man would willingly marry a Moabite.

On the way, Naomi attempts to get both of them to return back to Moab. It seems to be the sensible thing to do. Just like going to Moab, in the beginning, seemed to be the sensible thing to do when the famine hit. But the sensible thing is not always the right thing.

Proverbs 14:12 *"There is a way that seems right to a man, but its end is the way of death"*.

Naomi actually encouraged Ruth and Orpah to return to the gods of the Moabites. The Moabite god was Chemosh. The Moabite's sacrificed their children to this god! Naomi was actually suggesting that future happiness in marriage was worth forsaking what Ruth and Orpah had learned about the God of the Jews and return to child sacrificing! Naomi is disobeying another of God's covenant obligations.

Deuteronomy 13:6-10 *"If your brother, the son of your mother, your son or your daughter, the wife of your bosom, or your friend who is as your own soul, secretly entices you, saying, "Let us go and serve other gods, people which are all around you, near to you or far off from you, from one end of the earth to the other end of the earth, you shall not consent to him or listen to him, nor shall your eye pity him, nor shall you spare him or conceal him; but you shall surely kill him; your hand shall be first against him to put him to death, and afterward the hand of all the people. And you shall stone him with stones until he dies, because he sought to entice you away from the LORD your God, who brought you out of the land of Egypt, from the house of bondage."*

The word "return" in Hebrew is שׁוּב (shuv- pronounced shoove). This word also means "to repent and turn back". שׁוּב appears 12 times in Ruth 1:6-22. It is only found 3 times in the rest of the book and then only in reference to the journey recorded in the aforementioned passage. Numbers are important in Scriptures as well as names. The number 12 signifies Divine Authority. These twelve mentions of the word "Shuv" is telling the astute student of Scripture that this passage is about "repenting and returning to Divine Authority".

We began the chapter "in the days when the Judges ruled there was a famine". Disobedience to Divine Authority had brought about a famine. Now we are seeing a returning back to Divine Authority.

As Naomi is trying to get the two daughters-in-law to turn (shuv) back to Moab and to their god Chemosh, Ruth declares her allegiance to Divine Authority. This begins a startling contrast between

Naomi's and Ruth's response to the seemingly difficult times that life may bring. When Naomi faced destitution, death, and discouragement, she was content in disobeying the commandments of God. However, when Ruth is faced with destitution, death, and discouragement, she is determined to remain faithful to the God of Abraham and leave her family and her gods back in Moab.

Just before making the statement that exemplifies true commitment, the account tells us that Ruth "clave" (KJV) unto Naomi. Back in Genesis 2:24 Adam had said, *"Therefore shall a man leave his father and his mother, and shall cleave unto his wife: and they shall be one flesh"* (KJV). The same word for "cleave" in Genesis is the same word used for "clave" in the book of Ruth.

Ruth had married Naomi's son Mahlon. This meant more to Ruth than it did to Naomi. Ruth had a covenant relationship with her husband Mahlon and that extended to her mother-in-law as well. Ruth had left her family to marry Mahlon. Now she would leave her country, as well, to go wherever the mother of her deceased husband would go.

Ruth 1:16-17

"Entreat me not to leave you,
Or to turn back from following after you;
For wherever you go, I will go;
And wherever you lodge, I will lodge;
Your people shall be my people,
And your God, my God.
Where you die, I will die,
And there will I be buried.
The Lord do so to me, and more also,
If anything but death parts you and me."

Naomi blamed "the hand of Yahweh" (verse 13) for all her maladies, but Ruth says, "Your Elohim will be my Elohim". Later in verse 20 and 21, Naomi lays the full blame on El Shaddai (The God who is More Than Enough). Naomi asks to be called Mara (מָרָא) (pronounced Mar'-ah) which means bitter. Naomi was a bitter woman who blamed the One who she thought should have been "More Than

Enough" to her. Instead of blaming her own disobedience, Naomi was blaming God. The book of Ruth demonstrates vividly that obedience brings blessings while disobedience brings calamity.

However, Ruth shines brightly as one who is obedient to the Divine Authority. She demonstrates this through remaining with her mother-in-law and then continues it through working to provide for Naomi as well as herself. It matters not to Ruth whether her life is easy or hard. Ruth will <u>ALWAYS</u> obey God! We will see this even more as we continue through the narrative of the book of Ruth.

Now we come to the events that led up to the meeting and ultimate marriage of Ruth and Boaz. As we continue on our journey through this narrative, we will see how keeping covenant requirements are essential to receiving covenant blessings.

At this point, we might rightly ask ourselves, "What are the covenant requirements in my relationship with Yeshua (Jesus) that I need to reestablish in my life?" I assure you that in doing so you will open yourself up to covenant blessings above your imagination.

In Ruth 1:11-13 Naomi seems to be referring to the Levirate law when she says, *"If I should say I have hope, if I should have a husband tonight and should also bear sons, would you wait for them till they were grown?"* Naomi must have known at that time of the brothers of her dead husband. However, since she was too old to bear children, the Levirate law was no good to her. In addition, Naomi also realized that no Jewish man would willingly marry a Moabite woman, let alone a Moabite widow. Therefore, she encouraged Ruth and Orpah to return to Moab so that they could find husbands there.

Orpah says her goodbyes and returns, but Ruth clings to Naomi. At this point in the narrative, Ruth resigns herself to be a widow the rest of her life. Then a series of events unfold that change the course of history forever!

Ruth and Naomi return to Bethlehem without any visible means of support. The property that Naomi's husband Elimelech had is in someone else's possession. The property would not revert back to Naomi until the time of the Shemitah year.

The Shemitah is the Hebrew word for The Year of Jubilee. Every seven years any debt would be canceled and any property would be returned to the original owner.

Deuteronomy 15:1-2 *"At the end of every seven years you shall grant a release of debts. And this is the form of the release: Every creditor who has lent anything to his neighbor shall release it; he shall not require it of his neighbor or his brother, because it is called the LORD's release."*

Naomi and Ruth are destitute. However, there is provision made for the poor and the foreigner. They are allowed by law to glean the corners of the fields and get what little grain is left behind by the harvesters.

Leviticus 19:9 *"When you reap the harvest of your land, you shall not wholly reap the corners of your field, nor shall you gather the gleanings of your harvest. And you shall not glean your vineyard, nor shall you gather every grape of your vineyard; you shall leave them for the poor and the stranger: I am the LORD your God."*

Leviticus 23:22 *"When you reap the harvest of your land, you shall not wholly reap the corners of your field when you reap, nor shall you gather any gleaning from your harvest. You shall leave them for the poor and for the stranger: I am the LORD your God."*

Naomi is old and probably not able to go to the fields. Ruth takes on the responsibility and volunteers to work in the field and provide for herself as well as Naomi.

Ruth "happens" upon the field of Boaz. (We can see the Hand of God directing these events.) As Ruth is gleaning behind the reapers, Boaz comes out to the field. Boaz notices her because she seems out of place following the men who are reaping instead of the women. Therefore, he asks who she might be. When they tell him that she is the Moabitess who came with Naomi when she returned, Boaz went and spoke with Ruth.

Ruth 2:8 *"Then Boaz said to Ruth, "You will listen, my daughter, will you not? Do not go to glean in another field, nor go from here, but stay close by my young women."*

Here Boaz is directing Ruth as to the proper etiquette for gleaning. In Moab, it was perhaps permissible for women and men to work in close proximity of each other. This, however, was Israel and Ruth was sending a message to the young men that she did not intend to send.

Apparently, Boaz recognized his relationship to Ruth and wanted to do all he could to help her. All the while knowing that there was a nearer kinsman than himself, Boaz still wanted to do something. Ruth is curious as to his motivation for his kindness towards her. Boaz makes this statement:

Ruth 2:11-12 *"And Boaz answered and said to her, "It has been fully reported to me, all that you have done for your mother-in-law since the death of your husband, and how you have left your father and your mother and the land of your birth, and have come to a people whom you did not know before. The LORD repay your work, and a full reward be given you by the LORD God of Israel, under whose wings you have come for refuge."*

The word "wings" is the Hebrew word כָּנָף (pronounced "kah-nahf"). We learned this word in the chapter Under His Wings. It is translated corner, wing, hem, skirt, or lock (as in hair). Boaz says that Ruth is worthy of his kindness because of her covenant commitment to Naomi by leaving her mother and her father and coming to a people who are not her own. She had also made the God of Abraham her God. In so doing, she had come under His wings of protection. Boaz was simply allowing himself to be the instrument that God was using to bless Ruth for her obedience to the covenant.

Boaz went on to later leave "handfuls on purpose" for her. However, because Boaz knew that there was a "nearer kinsman", this was as much as he could do for Naomi and Ruth. Even if he wanted to do more, he was restricted by law.

Ruth returns to Naomi and tells her about her work day. Immediately Naomi realizes who Boaz is and informs Ruth. After the harvest, Naomi hatches a plan to bring Ruth and Boaz together.

Here is the plan. Ruth is to go to where Boaz is sleeping, guarding his grain. After Boaz goes to sleep, Ruth is to go and wake him up. The term "uncover his feet" in Ruth 3:4 is a euphemism for "wake him up".

110

However, Naomi is still trying to circumvent the covenant. There is a proper way to approach Boaz concerning the levirate law, but going in the middle of the night, with perfume and beautiful alluring clothes is not the way.

Naomi is suggesting something very similar to what Tamar did in alluring Judah. But there is a big difference between Judah and Boaz, as well as a big difference between Naomi and Ruth. Judah was violating covenant by not giving his son Shelah to Tamar. Boaz is a covenant keeping man. In fact, the workers give him a blessing and he returns the blessing as he visits his fields. By doing this He is connecting himself to Sinai and the giving of the commandments. Sinai was where God first gave the words of the Priestly blessing to Israel. (More on this Priestly Blessing in the chapter on Blessing.

Nevertheless, Ruth obeys her mother-in-law to a point. However, when she wakes up Boaz, Ruth is quick to make the assertion that he is a kinsman-redeemer a "go'el" in Hebrew (גאל). Then Ruth asks Boaz to "spread his skirt" over her. This was a request for Boaz to take the corner of his garment where Boaz would have his tzitzit tied and put it over Ruth. This would be a symbol of Ruth coming under the protection of Boaz as in a marriage proposal. Ruth's lying at his feet would signify that she was willing to be a servant to him as her future husband.

Ruth goes to great lengths to not appear to seduce Boaz. She only gives Boaz the suggestion that he be responsible to the Levirate law.

There was only one problem. There was an older brother who was a "nearer kinsman". Boaz met with him the next day and offered him the opportunity to redeem the land that Naomi had lost.

At first, this "nearer kinsman" was more than willing to purchase the land. However, when he learned that he would have to marry a Moabitess as part of the transaction, he suddenly had a change of heart. It seems that he did not want to damage his reputation by marrying a Gentile.

In this way, Boaz was free to marry Ruth and to give her a seed for her husband Mahlon. In so doing, he was in effect raising up a seed for his own brother Elimelech and fulfilling the levirate law.

So we have Boaz, who is a faithful covenant keeping man becoming a husband to Ruth who is a faithful covenant keeping woman. They produce a son by the name of Obed. If you remember, Obed means "Service and Worship". Obedience to God's covenant will always produce Service and Worship

Obed had a son by the name of Jesse, which means Yahweh exists! Service and Worship will bring us to the realization that Yahweh exists in the here and now. He is a present tense God. He is not the Great I was. Neither is He the Great I Will Be. But He is the Great I Am! Service and Worship make us aware of His working in our lives at this very moment. He is our healer today, not tomorrow. He is our provider today, not tomorrow. He is our deliverer today, not tomorrow. He is what we need today! He answers today. He provides today!

Jesse has a son by the name of David, which means "beloved". The reason Yahweh answers our every need today is because He loves us so very much! He answers our need because He wants us to enjoy being kings and priests on this earth.

And so we come to the end of the book of Ruth. But there is one more interesting point that can be made. If we view this story as an allegory, in some respects, we see an intriguing picture.

Let's assume, for the moment, that Ruth represents the Gentiles who come into covenant with the God of Abraham and are "grafted in" to the vine. Naomi then would represent Israel who was disobedient to the covenant and had lost her land and had been in exile in a foreign land.

It is Ruth, the Gentile, who shows Naomi, the Jewish people what true commitment to the covenant is all about. However, Ruth does not chide Naomi for her lack of commitment. Rather, she supports Naomi with her own labor and provides materially for her. It is directly related to her marriage to Boaz (a type of our Kinsman-Redeemer, Yeshua) that restores Naomi's land to her.

At this present moment in history, Jews are returning to their land and Christians (the Ruths of the world) are sending their own money, the fruits of their labors, in order to facilitate their return. It is because of our marriage to Yeshua that causes us to love His people.

But it is Naomi (Jewish people) who are teaching us about the roots of our own faith. We are learning about the prayer shawl, the tzitzit, the tekhelet thread, the shofar, the Hebrew names of God, the Tabernacle and many other things. We are beginning to see the walls of separation between us come down and we are becoming "one new man".

Chapter Eight
King Saul

I Samuel 15:27 (KJV) *"And as Samuel turned about to go away, he laid hold upon the skirt of his mantle, and it rent."*

Most translations and the majority of theologians interpret this verse to mean that as Samuel turned to leave, Saul grabbed the corner of Samuel's mantle and it tore. The sentence itself does not give us much clue as to whom is tearing the mantle. Even the Hebrew does not help.

I believe that the verse should be understood as *"And as Samuel turned about to go away, He,* (Samuel) *laid hold upon the skirt of his* (Saul's) *mantle, and it rent."* As we look at two different times that the skirt of Saul's mantle is torn or cut we can see a connection. This will validate my interpretation of this verse.

The word "skirt" in this passage is the Hebrew word "kanaph". As we studied earlier, this word means corner, wing, lock (as in hair), etc. Samuel would have torn the corner of Saul's mantle. On the corner of the mantle Saul would have had the tzitzit with the blue thread. When Samuel ripped the corner of the mantle, he did something very significant.

Among other things, the tzitzit on the corner of a garment represents authority. Kings, priests, prophets, and later Rabbis would fashion their tzitzit in a way that would set them apart from any other. You could recognize a person's tzitzit by its appearance. In fact, there are records of individuals of authority using their tzitzit to press into a sealing wax on a document to identify that document to them personally.

When Samuel ripped the tzitzit from King Saul, he said the following: *"The LORD has rent the kingdom of Israel from you this day, and has given it to a neighbor of yours, that is better than you."* At this point, Saul was not aware of who this person might be.

Now we look at the second time that King Saul had his tzitzit removed by someone. The account is in I Samuel chapter 24.

I Samuel 24: *"Then the men of David said to him, "This is the day of which the LORD said to you, "Behold, I will deliver your enemy into your hand, that you may do to him as it seems good to you." And David arose and secretly cut off a corner of Saul's robe. Now it happened afterward that*

118

David's heart troubled him because he had cut Saul's robe. And he said to his men, "The LORD forbid that I should do this thing to my master, the LORD's anointed, to stretch out my hand against him, seeing he is the anointed of the LORD."

Then we see Saul's response after David had shown him from a distance the tzitzit that he had cut off from the corner of Saul's mantle.

I Samuel 24:20 *"And now I know indeed that you shall surely be king, and that the kingdom of Israel shall be established in your hand. Therefore, swear now to me by the LORD that you will not cut off my descendants after me, and that you will not destroy my name from my father's house."*

Saul immediately made the connection between the words of Samuel when Samuel tore his mantle. Here was the "neighbor that is better" and he was holding the tzitzit (the symbol of his authority) in his hand. Saul realized that this was a fulfillment of the prophecy of Samuel. He realized at that moment that it was David who should replace him as king.

David's heart troubled him after he cut off the tzitzit from the corner of King Saul's mantle. David realized that what he did was an attack on the authority of the King of Israel. David recognized that though King Saul was out to kill him, David still had to respect the office of the King. The King was God's anointed.

The events leading up to these two scenes is very revealing. King Saul went from being anointed of God to being rejected by the very God who anointed him.

King Saul was told by God, through the Prophet Samuel, to completely destroy all the Amalekites. It was the Amalekites who had attacked the stragglers when Israel came out of Egypt. This was the prime moment that God would be able to completely rid Israel of this nation of people.

Saul disobeyed God. He kept the animals as well as Agag, the king of the Amalekites. Because he did this, a descendant of Agag, Haman the Agagite would nearly succeed in annihilating the Jewish people. You can read about this in the book of Esther.

119

Because of this error, Saul is rejected as being king. Samuel, in one swift move, tears his tzitzit off the corner of his mantle as a demonstration of his position being ripped from him.

This sets up the narrative where we will see how God's choice for the king is realized. However, the one who God chooses must first be tested. God uses King Saul to develop David for the role he is to play. One of the greatest moments is when David realizes that he has attacked the authority of God's anointed and he is troubled in his heart. This showed that David had great respect for the office of the King, and as such would respect the office after he is King. David respected and appreciated anointing.

Saul becoming king was quite an interesting part in the story of the "seed of woman". Saul was from the tribe of Benjamin. The promise of the scepter was to the tribe of Judah. Satan must have been really confused at this. But now it was becoming clearer. Satan only needed to find out the identity of this "neighbor" who was better than Saul and try to stop him.

Satan began immediately to work against the plan of God. He caused Jesse to not bring David to the prophet. He denied him the marriage to King Saul's daughter after killing Goliath. He motivates King Saul to throw a javelin at David, not once but twice! He feeds Saul with mistrust and causes him to hunt down David to kill him. Satan goes all out in his attempt to thwart God's choice of king.

Saul was the people's choice. God had always had a plan for a king for Israel. Ever since the prophecy of the scepter being in the tribe of Judah, God had been developing His king. Saul was out of God's timing.

Out on the hills of Judea, watching sheep, killing the lion and the bear, is God's man. David, the Psalmist, is going after God's heart. There in that wilderness, God and David are creating a lifelong relationship that will ultimately bring him into kingship.

Although David is the youngest of the family who is the direct descendant of Judah and Tamar, he is chosen over all his brothers. God chooses him because of his heart. God did not look at the outward appearance, God looked on David's heart.

You, like David, will be chosen for greatness not because of what you possess outwardly but because of what you possess inwardly. If your heart is right, he will pass over others more qualified than you. If your heart is right, he will elevate you in due time. Though you may face opposition, keep your heart right.

In the quietness of your lonely days, cultivate your relationship with God. Learn to sing during the lonely hours. Learn to fight the lions and the bears. One day, the Goliath that you will face and defeat will catapult you into your destiny!

The O.T. king and the O.T. prophet were to work hand in hand with each other. Under Moses and Joshua, God was king over the nation. However, after Joshua's death, Israel began to move away from God's direct authority over them. It became necessary for God to Send Judges to deliver them from time to time. It was during this time that Samuel arises as the last Judge of Israel. But Samuel was more than a Judge, he was a prophet.

When God gave in to the people's demand for a king (an earthly one), God realized that they had ultimately rejected Him and His authority over them. God allowed them to have a king, but He gave His prophets Divine direction for the king and the nation. If the king listened to the prophets, they would succeed and prosper (II Chronicles 20:20), if not they would falter and fail.

The N.T. antitype to the king is the Apostle. As long as the Apostle and the Prophet work together there is success and prosperity. We see this throughout the N.T. as well as in the present day. The fivefold ministry of Ephesians 4 is still valid today as it has been in the past.

The prayer shawl vividly demonstrates the prophet and king working together. The white of the tallit speaks of the priesthood, purity, and holiness. The tekhelet (blue) in the tzitzit speaks of the kingship. As the tzitzit hangs on to the corner of each white garment, so also does the king's authority hang on the corner of the prophet's purity and holiness.

In like manner, the Apostles ministry must be attached to and hang from the influence of the Prophet. Since the tallit is only a

121

spiritual garment when the tzitzit is attached, the Prophet's spiritual effectiveness is directly connected to the Apostle. Both need each other. Both give validity to each other's ministry. There is equality and interdependence in the Body of Christ.

The prayer shawl is abundant in teachings that are vital to our spiritual understandings. It is no wonder that I refer to this garment as *"The Teaching Tool Sent By God"*.

Chapter Nine
Elijah and Elisha

II *Kings 2:9-13 "And so it was, when they had crossed over, that Elijah said to Elisha, "Ask! What may I do for you, before I am taken away from you?"*

Elisha said, "Please let a double portion of your spirit be upon me."

So he said, "You have asked a hard thing. Nevertheless, if you see me when I am taken from you, it shall be so for you; but if not, it shall not be so." Then it happened, as they continued on and talked, that suddenly a chariot of fire appeared with horses of fire, and separated the two of them; and Elijah went up by a whirlwind into heaven.

And Elisha saw it, and he cried out, "My father, my father, the chariot of Israel and its horsemen!" So he saw him no more. And he took hold of his own clothes and tore them into two pieces. He also took up the mantle of Elijah that had fallen from him, and went back and stood by the bank of the Jordan."

This is a familiar scene that most of us have heard about many times. There is even at least one song that references this event specifically ("Swing low, sweet chariot. Comin' for to carry me home"). Some people see in this passage an example of "passing the mantle" of ministry from one individual to another.

In order to see the significance of this event and how it connects with the subject of this book, we will need to backtrack to where we are first introduced to Elijah. The narrative provides the background for our subject matter. You can read the story in its entirety in I Kings 17:1 through II Kings 2:15.

In I Kings 17:1 we are introduced to Elijah. He confronts King Ahab and informs him that it will not rain until Elijah says it will rain. Then for 3 ½ years, it does not rain.

During this period, God takes care of Elijah. First of all, he is fed by ravens by the brook Cherith. When the brook dries up due to the drought, God sends Elijah to a widow in Zarephath. God not only takes care of Elijah but He also miraculously takes care of the widow. When the widow's son dies, Elijah prays and brings him back to life.

Next, we find Elijah confronting Ahab again and challenging the 450 prophets of Baal and 400 prophets besides them to a

126

showdown on Mount Carmel. The contest is hilarious! The prophets of Baal fail to get their gods to answer by fire (or by any other means as well). Elijah, however, prays a simple prayer and God answers with dynamic power and fire comes and consumes the sacrifice. The people in unison make the declaration that Yahweh is Elohim! It seems that revival had come to Israel.

Then Elijah prays for rain and subsequently outruns Ahab's chariot going back to Jezreel (about 17 miles). At Jezreel, Ahab's wife Jezebel hears about what happened at Mount Carmel and how Elijah had all of the 450 prophets of Baal killed. Jezebel was not amused! Jezebel sends a messenger to Elijah to tell him that she would have him killed by the next day.

Elijah lets fear grip him and flees to Beersheba (about 70 miles away). Elijah leaves his servant at Beersheba and then goes another day's journey and collapses under a broom bush (Juniper tree is in the King James Version, but is inaccurate. The Hebrew word is actually a broom bush).

Now, let's leave Elijah under this broom bush for the moment. There is another time that someone was put under a broom bush in this very location!

Genesis 21:14-16 *"So Abraham rose early in the morning, and took bread and a skin of water; and putting it on her shoulder, he gave it and the boy to Hagar, and sent her away. Then she departed and wandered in the Wilderness of Beersheba. And the water in the skin was used up, and she placed the boy under one of the shrubs. Then she went and sat down across from him at a distance of about a bowshot; for she said to herself, "Let me not see the death of the boy." So she sat opposite him, and lifted her voice and wept."*

Here is Hagar with her son Ishmael. Hagar is faced with death. Could it be that Elijah purposely went to this very spot near Beersheba and maybe picked out the very bush that Ishmael had been under?

I believe that Elijah was feeling abandoned by God just as Hagar and Ismael had been abandoned by Abraham. After having such an amazing work of God on Mount Carmel, it would only seem

127

natural that God would finish what he started and revival would sweep the land of Israel. Instead of that happening, Jezebel was seeking his life! All Mount Carmel did was to put a bullseye on the back of Elijah. God got him into this mess and now God has abandoned him! So, just as Hagar thrust her child under the bush in order for him to die, Elijah thrust himself under the bush and ask God to kill him.

Obviously, if Elijah really wanted to die, he could have stayed in Jezreel and Jezebel would have obliged him without a problem. Elijah didn't want to die. His request to die is really a complaint to God. Elijah says in I Kings 19:4 *"It is enough! Now, LORD, take my life, for I am no better than my fathers!"* Listen to Elijah's complaint! "I have had enough! Just kill me now! I am no better than my fathers, Abraham, Isaac, and Jacob! Since you have abandoned me (like Abraham abandoned Ishmael in this very spot under this very bush) just go ahead and finish the job and kill me now."

This is so like most of us, we reach the point in our service for the Lord that we are done. We have had enough of the problems, enough of the heartaches, enough of the opposition. Lord, just let me die! When we get this way, it is because deep down we feel that God has abandoned us. After all, didn't it look like victory was assured and the battle was finally over? After all, our entire energy was put into the success of the last encounter with the forces of satan and we came out on top! Why is it not over? I can't face another battle. Just take me now!

This is Elijah, a man of like passions as you and I. He lays himself under the broom bush and goes to sleep. He is done. He is through. He has had enough.

God won't leave Elijah alone, and my friend God will not leave you alone either. An angel came and woke Elijah up. This angel is identified later as the Angel of Yahweh. The Angel of Yahweh is none other than Yeshua (Jesus) in a pre-incarnate appearance.

The Angel (Yeshua) says to Elijah, "get up and eat". Elijah eats the cake and drinks the water and then goes back to sleep. A little later, the Angel (Yeshua) wakes him up again and has him eat and drink again. Elijah goes on the strength of those two meals for 40 days and 40 nights!

It seems that he is being led to Mount Horeb by the Spirit of God. Normally, he could make the trip of approximately 200 miles in about two weeks. Why does it take him 40 days?

The number 40 is significant and it is not an accident that it is mentioned here. 40 is the number of testing, trial, or probation. It also indicates transition or change; the concept of renewal; a new beginning. Elijah goes for 40 days and 40 nights and he is about to experience a transition and change in his ministry.

Mount Horeb is also known by another name, Mount Sinai. If you remember, the children of Israel wandered for 40 years in the wilderness before reaching Canaan. Like those children of Israel of old Elijah is wandering in the wilderness, probably unaware that God is ultimately taking him to Mount Sinai.

Why Sinai? What is God doing with Elijah? What does Sinai tell us about God's dealing with Elijah?

Mount Sinai (Mount Horeb) is where Moses met with the Angel of Yahweh at the burning bush (probably the same type of bush that Elijah had wished to die under back in the wilderness of Beersheba). Moses, at Sinai, had received new direction from God to deliver the Israelites from slavery. Now the Israelites were under a different type of slavery. Jezebel and Ahab had put Israel under the slavery of Baal worship.

It was to Mount Sinai that Moses, by God's leading, brought the newly liberated Israelites. It was on Mount Sinai that the mountain was full of smoke (where there is smoke, there is fire) and lightning and earthquakes. It was at Mount Sinai where Moses had asked to see God's face and God hid him in a "cleft of the rock" and passed by where Moses could see His backsides. It was at Mount Sinai that Moses was 40 days on the mountain receiving the Ten Commandments that made them into a nation. It was at Mount Sinai that Moses received commandment for the Tabernacle as well as for the Tzitzit that was to be worn on the corners of their garments.

Mount Sinai was a place of direction, instruction, closeness to God, deliverance, and transition from slavery to interdependence on God. It was a place for a national revival. Israel had been revived after over 400 years of slavery. Elijah must have been struck at the wonder of the possibility of what God had in mind by bringing him here.

We see Elijah in a cave. Actually, the Hebrew words here signify that Elijah was in "the" cave (I Kings 19:9). המערה is the Hebrew word for "the cave". When the letter ה (Hay) is added to the front of a word it is translated as the definite article "the". Elijah wasn't in just any cave; he was in a very specific cave. This cave was probably the same placed described as the "cleft of the rock" that Moses was placed many years before.

The wind, fire, and earthquake that Elijah experienced were reminiscent of the manifestations of God on Mount Sinai when the Commandments were given. However, God was not in the wind, fire, or earthquake! God was about to reveal something to Elijah. How God dealt with people in the past was not going to be the way he deals with people today. There will be a transition, a change. God is going to deliver in a completely different manner than before. The battle with Jezebel and her prophets of Baal is a different type of battle than with Pharaoh.

With Pharaoh, God delivered with "a mighty hand". With Pharaoh, God brought 10 plagues on Egypt and decimated everything. With Pharaoh, God's people were in a foreign land with other gods. This was different. Now, foreign gods were in the land of God's people.

Mount Carmel was only phase one of God's plan to deliver His people from Baal and Jezebel. As we shall see God had 4 more phases in His plan of deliverance. These combined make a total of 5 phases to defeat Baal and Jezebel.

5 is the number of grace. Now, you may have heard that grace means "unmerited favor". Let me tell you that is not entirely true. The word "grace" in the Greek is χάρις (charis – pronounced kah'-reese). It can mean several things such as "gifts" (as in spiritual gifts) and even "unmerited favor". However, it may also mean "Divine enablement"

as in I Corinthians 15:10, II Corinthians 12:9, II Timothy 2:1, and I Peter 4:10. If you replace the word "grace" in these passages with the definition of "Divine enablement", you will find that it makes a clearer thought than with the definition of "gift" or "unmerited favor".

God was revealing to Elijah through the number 5 that He was going to deliver Israel from the power of Baal and Jezebel by His Divine enablement through the remaining 4 phases of His plan.

We have the wind, fire, and earthquake and it specifically states that God was not in the wind, fire, or earthquake. Then, there was a "still, small voice". The Hebrew literally says, *"sound of a gentle stillness"*. This would have been a silence that was filled with the very Presence of God. It was in this awesome stillness that the Presence of God was so profound that Elijah recognized immediately the sanctity of the moment and wrapped his mantle (with tzitzit attached) around his face.

This is the first time that we see Elijah doing anything with his "mantle". The mantle plays an important role in his life from this day forward. Much like the shepherd's staff that Moses had that God turned into a miracle staff, Elijah's mantle becomes a miracle mantle.

When Elijah in this Holy silence recognized the Presence of God, he wrapped his face in his mantle. This would have been a garment with four corners on which would have been tied the tzitzit. This was a forerunner of the present day Jewish prayer shawl. Elijah closed himself in with God into the "secret place", his personal "Holy of Holies where God would meet with him.

There in that cave, with his mantle wrapped around his face, God gives Elijah the rest of the plan. The following are the 5 phases of God's plan to eradicate Baal worship along with Jezebel and her husband King Ahab.

1.   Defeat Baal at Mount Carmel and turn the attention of the people back to God. (This has already been accomplished.)

2.   Anoint Hazael as king of Syria

3.   Anoint Jehu as king of Israel

4. Anoint Elisha as your successor

5. There are 7000 that have not bowed their knees to Baal.

The order that God would use these 4 remaining phases is different than what the text gives us. As we see in the narrative, the first thing Elijah does is to anoint Elisha. In fact, Hazael and Jehu do not show up until after Elijah goes to heaven.

What about the 7000? Where do they fit in? What is their part in God's plan? Other than encouraging Elijah, why does God mention them? As we shall see these 7000 play a vital part in the defeat of Jezebel and her prophets of Baal.

The number 7 and the number 1000 are both numbers of completion. Jewish teaching verifies that there are 7000 years of God's dealing with the earth that corresponds to the 7 days of creation. At the end of 6000 years, we will enter into 1000 years of peace with Messiah ruling from Jerusalem. The number 7000 said to Elijah that peace was returning to Israel and that God was still in control. Jezebel has not won the day. God Himself is still on the throne.

Elijah has renewed vision. Elijah has been infused with Godly enthusiasm. Elijah is ready to get back into the ministry that God has called him into. He is no longer in the bush or hiding in a cave. Elijah comes out into the open. He is no longer afraid of Jezebel. There are 7000 that have not bowed the knee! There is power in numbers! Elijah is not alone! This fact has the power to encourage Elijah and give him a new vision and renewed energy.

Most of the time God's presence is enough. However, there are times that we want something more tangible. A story is told of a young girl who was very scared and asked her mom to come to her room. Her mother, trying to calm her daughter, told her that she had nothing to fear, God was in her room. To which the little girl replied, I don't want God, I want something with skin on! The greatest encouragement to Elijah was that there were 7000 who had "skin on". God's presence is fine, but there is just something about having the support of others in the work.

132

Elijah immediately goes and finds Elisha. Elisha is plowing with 12 yokes of oxen and he is with the 12th. The number 12 speaks of Apostolic authority and government. This immediately makes me think of the 12 Apostles that were called by Yeshua.

Elijah casts his mantle (with tzitzit attached) over Elisha. Elisha understands what this means. He does not need anyone to explain it to him. Just as Ruth had asked Boaz to put the corner of his garment over her to demonstrate his willingness to have a covenant relationship, so Elijah is expressing this same willingness to Elisha by putting his mantle (with tzitzit attached) over him.

Elijah was saying to Elisha, "Come under my wing. Let me teach you. Become my disciple."

Elisha immediately responded and ran after Elijah. After saying goodbye to his father and mother and preparing a feast for his former employees, he left it all and followed Elijah.

When Yeshua called his disciples, He said to them "follow me". I wonder, knowing the implications of placing a mantle (with tzitzit attached) over a prospective student, if Yeshua might have placed His prayer shawl over the shoulders of those whom he called. There is nothing in the New Testament narrative to suggest any such thing, but it is an interesting question. This would explain perhaps why those whom Yeshua called were immediately willing to leave their livelihoods and come "under His wing".

Elisha was not the first disciple of Elijah. Back in Beersheba, Elijah had left his servant in Beersheba before going a day's journey into the wilderness to throw himself under a broom bush (I Kings 19:3). But, as we shall see when Elijah is taken up into heaven, Elisha is quite a different servant than the first one.

The text does not give us the specifics of what transpired between Elijah and Elisha during the ensuing months and years. However, we do read of a "school of the prophets" in several locations. Reading between the lines, we might suppose that those 7000 who had not bowed their knees to Baal might be the "students" in these schools.

The students in these schools would have been emboldened by what happened at Mount Carmel to come out of their secret places and join with Elijah who obviously was the leader of these schools. They would be established to not only teach the prophetic to these students but would also provide a means for intercession for the revival that was to come. It seems that these schools had a measure of safety because Jezebel is not recorded as attacking them as she had the prophets of Yahweh before.

When Elijah came down from Mount Sinai with his "miracle mantle" things had changed in the land. A movement was beginning to form. God was organizing a prayer army to usher in revival.

The remaining phases of God's deliverance do not take place until after Elijah is taken into heaven. The anointing of Hazael and Jehu will be left to Elisha.

(The events that lead to the final demise of Ahab, his sons, and his wife Jezebel, along with the worship of Baal, is beyond the scope of this book. After reading this chapter, you may want to follow the story in your own personal study.)

Elijah is made aware that God wants to take him home. Apparently, Elisha, as well as the other students, knew as well. This brings us to a very interesting part of the narrative of Elijah and Elisha.

Elijah and Elisha are about to take a circular journey through four locations where there is a school of the prophets at each one.

While this could be simply Elijah's farewell to each of the schools and the students at those locations; spiritually, these four locations have great significance for us who are looking for a double portion as Elisha was that day.

II Kings 2:1-9 *"And it came to pass, when the LORD was about to take up Elijah into heaven by a whirlwind, that Elijah went with Elisha from Gilgal. Then Elijah said to Elisha, "Stay here, please, for the LORD has sent me on to Bethel."*

But Elisha said, "As the LORD lives, and as your soul lives, I will not leave you!" So they went down to Bethel.

Now the sons of the prophets who were at Bethel came out to Elisha, and said to him, "Do you know that the LORD will take away your master from over you today?"

And he said, "Yes, I know; keep silent!"

Then Elijah said to him, "Elisha, stay here, please, for the LORD has sent me on to Jericho."

But he said, "As the LORD lives, and as your soul lives, I will not leave you!" So they came to Jericho.

Now the sons of the prophets who were at Jericho came to Elisha and said to him, "Do you know that the LORD will take away your master from over you today?"

So he answered, "Yes, I know; keep silent!"

Then Elijah said to him, "Stay here, please, for the LORD has sent me on to the Jordan."

But he said, "As the LORD lives, and as your soul lives, I will not leave you!" So the two of them went on.

And fifty men of the sons of the prophets went and stood facing them at a distance, while the two of them stood by the Jordan.

Now Elijah took his mantle, rolled it up, and struck the water; and it was divided this way and that, so that the two of them crossed over on dry ground.

And so it was, when they had crossed over, that Elijah said to Elisha, "Ask! What may I do for you, before I am taken away from you?"

Elisha said, "Please let a double portion of your spirit be upon me."

The four locations mentioned in the passage are Gilgal, Bethel, Jericho, and Jordan. Before we look at the significance of these four places, let us investigate what Elisha was asking when he said to Elijah, *"Please let a double portion of your spirit be upon me."*

The concept of the double portion is first mentioned in Deuteronomy 21:17 *"But he shall acknowledge the son of the unloved wife as the firstborn by giving him a double portion of all that he has, for he is the beginning of his strength; the right of the firstborn is his."*

The law of Deuteronomy says that the first son should be the one that receives the double portion blessing. Elisha is not Elijah's son, but Elisha is asking God to give him something that breaks protocol. In other words, when there is prophecy over your life, it exceeds protocol!

Look at these examples in Scripture. Jacob is chosen over Esau. Judah is chosen over Reuben, Simeon, and Levi, all who are older than him. Ephraim was chosen over Manasseh. There were times that God broke protocol and sanctioned the blessing of a younger over the older with the double portion.

God had intended for the Jewish people as a nation to follow Yeshua and receive the double portion. However, like the first servant who left Elijah and stayed in Beersheba, Israel would not follow Yeshua. Then comes the Gentiles who, like Elisha, follow Yeshua and receive the double portion that Israel rejected. However, all Gentiles did not receive the double portion, for there were those who stayed at Gilgal, Bethel, Jericho, and would not cross Jordan, but viewed afar off.

Therefore, the double portion belongs to the one who will continue to follow and not be persuaded to remain content at each of the four locations.

It is obvious that Elisha's request was simply a request for the right of the firstborn son, which would have meant that Elisha would be recognized as Elijah's successor. However, Elisha got more than what he asked for. We notice that over Elisha's life he had twice as many miracles as Elijah.

The following shows the miracles of Elijah and Elisha, respectfully.

Elijah's Eight Miracles

From First and Second Kings

1. Shutting heaven and stopping the rain for three years. (I Kings 17:1)
2. Oil multiplied, the grain increased daily, the widow woman. (I Kings 17:2)

3. Widow's son raised from the dead. (I Kings 17:22)
4. Fire from heaven on the soaked altar. (I Kings 18:38)
5. Rain returns. (I Kings 18:45)
6. The fire brought down on 51 soldiers. (II Kings 1:10)
7. The fire brought down on the second 51 soldiers (II Kings 1:12)
8. The parting of the river Jordan. (II Kings 2:8)

Elisha's Sixteen Miracles
From the Second Book of Kings

1. Jordan river divided. (2:14)
2. Waters at the spring of Jericho healed. (2:21)
3. Bears from the woods, destroying the mockers. (2:24)
4. Water for kings. (3:20)
5. Oil for the widow. (4:1-4)
6. Gift of a son (4:16, 17)
7. Raising the child from the dead. (4:35)
8. Healing of the pottage. (4:41)
9. Bread multiplied. (4:43)
10. Naaman healed. (5:10)
11. Gehazi smitten with leprosy. (5:27)
12. Caused the iron to swim. (6:6)
13. Spiritual sight to his servant. (6:17)
14. Smiting blindness to men (6:18)
15. Restoring sight to these same men. (6:20)
16. The miracle after his death, a man comes to life by touching Elisha's bones. (13:21)

This would be in accordance with Scriptures related to the double portion. In the following examples we see the double portion meaning: "a double quantity of something"

- Hannah received a "double portion" from her husband "because he loved her" (I Samuel 21:17).

- Isaiah 61:7 promises a double portion of joy and blessing to Israel.

- God restored to Job twice as much as he had before his time of testing. (Job 42:10)

- Prior to the Sabbath, they were to receive twice as much manna when they were in the wilderness (Exodus 16:22, 29). Among other things, the Sabbath points to the 1,000-year reign of Christ after 6,000 years of man's rule on this earth. This signifies to us that just prior to this millennial reign, there would be a double portion of His spirit poured out on the earth.

- Hosea, Joel, and James, the brother of Yeshua all speak of a double portion that will be poured out on the earth in the last days.

  o Hosea 6:2-3 *"After two days* **(this is the two days or 2,000 years of the church age)** *He will revive us; On the third day He will raise us up, that we may live in His sight. Let us know, let us pursue the knowledge of the LORD. His going forth is established as the morning; He will come to us like the rain, Like the latter and former rain to the earth."*

  o Joel 2:23 *"Be glad then, you children of Zion, And rejoice in the LORD your God; for He has given you the former rain faithfully, and He will cause the rain to come down for you — The former rain, and the latter rain in the first month."*

  The former rain was on the day of Pentecost. The latter rain was at the turn of the century with the outpouring of the Spirit of God throughout the world from a small building on Azusa Street in California.

  The former rain was entirely Jewish; the latter rain was predominately Gentile. However, this last great outpouring will be upon Jew and Gentile alike. Thus, we shall see the "one new man" that is mentioned in Ephesians 2:14-16.

138

The Gentile church needs the Jewish people and their understanding of the Old Testament and the Jewish people need the Gentile church and their understanding of the New Testament. God is going to pour out his Spirit and make us both one in these last days.

o   James 5:7 *"Therefore be patient, brethren, until the coming of the Lord. See how the farmer waits for the precious fruit of the earth, waiting patiently for it until it receives the early and latter rain."*

There is a harvest, but prior to the harvest, there must be the early and latter rain. We are to wait patiently for it. This is not a passive waiting. This is an expectant waiting! The rain is about to fall! Can you see it? I can see a cloud about the size of a man's hand! I can hear the sound of the abundance of rain! It is the double portion!

I want to point out one more place where we see the double portion. In the Tabernacle of Moses, we have three separate compartments for worship. We have the Outer Court, the Holy Place, and the Holy of Holies.

In the Outer Court, we have two instruments of worship – the Brazen Altar and the Laver. In the Holy Place, we have three instruments of worship – the Candlestick, the Table of Showbread, and the Altar of Incense.

However, in the Holy of Holies, we have twice as many instruments of worship as we did in the Holy Place. In the Holy of Holies, we have six instruments of worship – Aaron's Rod that Budded, the Golden Pot of Manna, the Ten Commandments, the Ark of the Covenant, the Mercy Seat, and the Cherubim over the Mercy Seat.

The Holy of Holies is the place of the double portion! When you wrap your prayer shawl around your head, you enter into your own personal Holy of Holies and experience the benefits of the double portion!

Returning now to our examination of the text concerning Elisha's request, we will now look at the four places that Elisha and Elijah traveled through prior to Elijah's departure and Elisha's receiving the double portion.

The following map of Israel at the time of Elijah may be beneficial in order for you to see the correlation of these four places.

The first place is Gilgal. This is the starting point. Apparently, this was where they both lived. Gilgal may well have been the first school that was founded. As such, it would be the foundation or basis for the teaching at the other schools at Bethel and Jericho.

The name Gilgal means "rolling". We encounter Gilgal in Joshua 5:9 *"Then the LORD said to Joshua, "This day I have rolled away the reproach of Egypt from you." Therefore, the name of the place is called Gilgal to this day."*

What is "the reproach of Egypt" talking about in this verse? The reproach was "rolled away" by the Jordan rolling back and the subsequent circumcision of all those that were born during the 40 years of wandering.

This phrase refers to a scenario Moses had raised with God in his several intercessory prayers (Exodus 32:12; Numbers 14:13-16; Deuteronomy 9:28). If Israel perished in the wilderness, Moses had argued, the Egyptians would hear about it. They would reason that though God had delivered Israel out of Egypt, He had not been powerful enough to bring them safely through the wilderness. This would bring reproach not only upon Israel but also upon God.

The rolling back of Jordan, so the Israelites could cross over into the promised land took away the reproach that the Egyptians would have had toward them and their God.

The circumcision was their part of rolling off the reproach of Egypt from themselves. By this act, they were declaring that they were separate from other men. They belonged only to God. No longer were they slaves; they were free to be servants of God. All the while during the 40 years of wandering, the Israelites continually stated their desire to return to Egypt. This generation was declaring their independence as well as their desire to never serve anyone except Yahweh ever again.

It is at Gilgal that God delivers you from the influence of Egypt. It matters not to you what the world may say, you are separated unto God. His opinion is the only opinion that matters. Your heart has been circumcised. Your heart only belongs to God.

Gilgal is a place of stripping. Everything that you have leaned on in the past is stripped away. At Gilgal, there is no more cloud by day and fire by night to lead you. At Gilgal, there is no more manna. From now on the people would have to sow and reap for themselves. Gilgal represents a life of faith.

At Gilgal, you are stripped of your finances, stripped of your health, stripped of relationships. At Gilgal, you are stripped of your support system. When you ask others to pray for you, nothing happens. You are left on your own to believe God for yourself. You must work for your healing, confessing the Word over your body. You have to work for your finances, confessing the Word over your sources of income. You have to work for relationships, confessing the Word over your family and your friends. Nothing comes easy now. You have to keep the weeds from growing by watching your idle words. You have to give the seed of the Word of God time to germinate and sprout and grow into what you are speaking that Word over. In the meantime, you have to learn patience, the ability to stay the same regardless of situations or circumstances. At Gilgal, you have to let patience have its perfect work, wanting nothing (James 1:4).

Before Gilgal, you depended on the prayer and the faith of your pastor or the elders of the church. But in order to qualify for the double portion, you will have to take the Word of God in your mouth yourself. You will have to speak over your own life and "call things that be not as though they are".

Before Gilgal, you could live on the "saucer blessings" that spilled over from another's faith. At Gilgal, you will have to sow before you reap. You will have to cultivate that which is sown. You will have to stand and keep on standing even after you have done all to stand.

Gilgal is where you learn that it is "through faith and patience that you receive the promise". Gilgal is where you declare your independence as well as your complete dependence on God and God alone.

There are some who have never even come to Gilgal, let alone go on to the other three locations. There are those who are still immature and still on the "milk of the word". There are some who still depend on someone more spiritual to feed them, burp them, and change their diapers.

Those that are at Gilgal know the excitement of a life of faith. Those at Gilgal know the freedom of being dependent on God alone. Those at Gilgal experience a personal closeness to their Creator that none other knows about.

It is tempting to stay at Gilgal and not go on to receive the double portion. There are many who are satisfied to remain at Gilgal. Many are stuck at Gilgal. They even begin faith ministries to teach others faith. They know no other diet. They are constantly speaking about their faith. "By faith" is their byword. They have more faith in their own faith than they have in God. They are constantly looking for a formula. When someone sows a plane and reaps a jet, they give away their only automobile, expecting to receive a better one.

Gilgal will eventually make you materialistic instead of Spiritual. Gilgal will destroy you in the end if you stay there. Gilgal is a wonderful place to visit, but you don't want to stay there.

Elijah tries to get Elisha to stay at Gilgal. Elijah wants to know if Elisha will be like his first servant who was content to stay at Beersheba while he went into the wilderness to die. Now that Elijah is going to be taken away, he tries to dissuade Elisha from following him to Bethel. However, Elisha has a greater goal than simply a life of faith. He wants more than materialism. He wants more than health. He wants more than family and friends. Elisha wants the double portion.

For Elisha, it is a covenant relationship with Elijah. He is more interested in his relationship with Elijah than he is with what he can receive at Gilgal. It is Elijah who is the center of his attention. He will not leave Him. Like Ruth and Naomi of old, Elisha is attached at the hip to Elijah.

Our Elijah, Yeshua, is moving from Gilgal to Bethel, will we follow him or will we remain where we are? Will we go on with the Lord? Is our relationship with our Lord and Savior more important than the things we receive at his hand? Can we leave all the blessings we worked so hard for at Gilgal to go on to Bethel? I pray we do!

Bethel is the second most mentioned place in the Bible. Only Jerusalem is mentioned more times. Therefore, Bethel becomes a significant place not only in the Word of God but also in our own lives.

The name Bethel means "House of God". It was at Bethel that Jacob came when he was running away from his brother Esau. It was at Bethel that Jacob had his dream of a ladder going to heaven with angels ascending and descending on it. It was at Bethel that God reminded Jacob of his new name that he received after wrestling with the Angel at the river Jabbok.

It was at Bethel that Abraham built an altar and called upon the name of the Lord. Bethel has some of the highest peaks in the land of Israel. Bethel also is a place where there are many springs of water. It was at Bethel that Lot looked out and saw the plains of Jordan that they were well watered and left to pitch his tent near Sodom and Gomorrah. It was also at this same Bethel that God told Abraham to look North, South, East, and West for all the land that he sees God would give him.

From Bethel, you can see as far north as Mount Hermon and the peaks of upper Galilee. To the South, you can see the hills of Hebron and the Negev. To the West, you can see the coastal plain. To the East, you can see the Jordan valley, the hills of Gilead, and the mountains of Moab in eastern Transjordan.

It was at Bethel that Deborah lived and judged Israel. It was at Bethel that a future King Saul would prophesy so much that they would exclaim, "Is Saul also among the prophets?" Very soon, after Bethel, Saul would embrace his destiny as the first king of Israel.

It was at Bethel that Jeroboam erected a golden calf (another one was erected in Dan). Jeroboam wanted to create a separate place of worship instead of Jerusalem because of the divided kingdom after the death of Solomon. Jeroboam must have chosen this particular place because of his knowledge of Jacob's ladder and the open heaven.

Bethel is the place of dreams and a change of names. It is a place of a change of destiny. Names in the Bible were often prophetic of the destiny of an individual. Your name shaped your life and your future.

However, dreams come with a price. There must be a Jabbok. There must be a wrestling. There must be a change. That old Jacob spirit has to die. It is a place where you are face to face with God and you give Him everything, spirit, soul, and body.

Some succeed at Bethel, others fail. It is a place of surrender, yielding, a place of dying to your desires and getting a God-given dream. It is the place of an open heaven where the prophetic comes over your life. It is a place where you expand your horizon and embrace your destiny. You look to the East, West, North, and South and claim your inheritance.

You will meet the greatest opposition to your dreams and destiny here at Bethel. Your own peers and your family will come and try to steal your dream and they will continue to follow you into

Jericho and also Jordan. But they will never join you. They are there only to discourage you. "Don't you know that the Lord is going to take away your master today?" What are you going to do then? You are nothing without him. What will happen to your ideas of grandeur then? Do you really think that you will become his successor? No one can replace Elijah!

Look what Elisha says, "Hold your peace". I know Elijah is going to be taken today. However, I know something you do not know. There is a mantle. I am not sure about how this all works, but there is something miraculous about that mantle. I know that the mantle will make all the difference.

Then, Elijah, himself tells you to stay at Bethel because he is going to Jericho. But you cannot be discouraged, you cannot be deterred, you have only one goal in mind, getting that mantle (with tzitzit attached).

Bethel is a great mountain top experience! It is tempting to stay here. It is glorious! It is wonderful! It is exciting! But our Elijah is going on to Jericho and we must follow if we want his mantle. We must now go down into the valley.

Jericho is the lowest city on the planet. It sits 846 feet below sea level. The name Jericho in Hebrew means fragrant. Jericho is surrounded by palm trees which bear dates. The palm trees survive because there are underground springs that keep them watered. This is a picture of present-day Jericho.

Near Jericho is the valley of the shadow of death that David talked about in Psalm 23. It was on the road to Jericho that Zacchaeus climbed into a sycamore tree to get a better view of Yeshua passing by. It was also on this road that blind Bartimaeus cried out to Yeshua

145

"Have mercy on me". Yeshua healed his blind eyes. The road to Jericho was the setting for the parable of the good Samaritan.

However, Jericho is better remembered for the battle that was won there by Joshua. Joshua's strategy for the military campaign to conquer Canaan was to divide and conquer. By taking Jericho and Ai, he could continue westward and place his army directly across the center of the land. This would separate the enemy to the south from the enemy in the north. Once he was able to subdue the southern armies, he could then turn his attention to the armies farther north. It was a plan that General Allenby of England copied in World War I in nearly the same area when England conquered Palestine from the Ottoman Turks.

Joshua won the battle at Jericho because he turned over his position of leader to the man with the sword and followed His plan (Joshua 5:13-14). Revelation 19:11-16 describes this man again.

"Now I saw heaven opened, and behold, a white horse. And He who sat on him was called Faithful and True, and in righteousness He judges and makes war. His eyes were like a flame of fire, and on His head were many crowns. He had a name written that no one knew except Himself. He was clothed with a robe dipped in blood, and His name is called The Word of God. And the armies in heaven, clothed in fine linen, white and clean, followed Him on white horses. Now out of His mouth goes a sharp sword, that with it He should strike the nations. And He Himself will rule them with a rod of iron. He Himself treads the winepress of the fierceness and wrath of Almighty God. And He has on His robe and on His thigh a name written;

KING OF KINGS AND
LORD OF LORDS."

This man with the sword drawn was none other than Yeshua. Joshua followed his orders fully. Therefore, we see that Jericho is not only a place of spiritual warfare, but also a place of yielding our every thought over to the one with the sword drawn.

Jericho is where you will fight your greatest battles. You have come from Gilgal where you learned about faith. You then went to Bethel where you were on the mountain top in the presence of the

Lord and received your heavenly vision. Now your faith and your dreams are going to be attacked like never before! Spiritual warfare is your next step in getting the mantle.

At Jericho, you will encounter walls that are so formidable that the very sight of them will cause you to lose hope. At Jericho, you will not be far from the valley of the shadow of death. It will appear that your hopes and dreams will not be realized. It will appear that your dreams are not real. Like Joseph in prison, you may forget you ever had a dream.

Nevertheless, at Jericho, you are not alone. There is one with a sword drawn who will give you the victory provided you will submit every thought to him and follow his leadership.

This battle will not be won by carnal means. This is a spiritual battle that needs supernatural weapons. As it says in II Corinthians 10:4-6

"For the weapons of our warfare are not carnal but mighty in God for pulling down strongholds, casting down arguments and every high thing that exalts itself against the knowledge of God, bringing every thought into captivity to the obedience of Christ, and being ready to punish all disobedience when your obedience is fulfilled."

This is a battle of the mind. Yeshua told Joshua "Look! I have given you Jericho." Joshua looked at Jericho and had to submit his thoughts to what Yeshua had said. He could no longer see the wall. He had to look at the wall the way Yeshua saw the wall.

At Gilgal, the place of faith, you gave your heart. At Bethel, the place of dreams, you gave your spirit, soul, and body. Now at Jericho, you give your very thoughts. This is all preparing you for the double portion. This is what it is going to take to get the mantle.

It is hard to leave Jericho. You are tired. Surely, we have done enough. Maybe we can just rest here in the fragrance of the victory. After all, isn't fragrance what Jericho really represents? After all, fragrance is what Jericho means in Hebrew!

Staying at Jericho cannot be for there is a curse on Jericho. Sure victory smells sweet, but beware building at Jericho. Didn't Joshua curse Jericho and say that if anyone tried to build this city they would lay the foundation in the death of their first son and would finish it in the death of their youngest son? (Joshua 6:26)

Nevertheless, there will be those who do not want you to go on. There will be those who do not believe you deserve the double portion. In fact, the reason they do not believe you deserve it is because they believe they do not deserve it. They have accepted something less because they believed they did not deserve anything more.

Even Elijah is requesting that you stop following him and stay. Elijah is going to Jordan. It is all right with him if you do not go. He will not force you to go any further if you do not want to go.

But you want that mantle (with tzitzit attached)! You want more! You are not sure you deserve it, but that does not matter. You want it! Something pushes you on. It is a calling that has overtaken your life ever since Elijah cast his mantle (with tzitzit attached) on you when you were plowing the field. You will follow all the way to Jordan and beyond.

Your passion has stirred up 50 of the students at Jericho and they start to follow. But when they get close to Jordan, they hang back. They become spectators to the happenings at Jordan, but they do not participate.

You two will go on to the banks of the Jordan river. There at that river you will face one final test.

Jordan is where Joshua told the priests who bore the Ark of the Covenant to stand while the people of Israel passed over on dry land. Jordan is where they took 12 stones to put at Gilgal and 12 stones to be put in the middle of Jordan. Jordan is where Naaman was healed of leprosy after dipping 7 times. Jordan is where John the Baptist baptized. Jordan is where Yeshua was baptized by John prior to beginning His ministry.

John's baptism wasn't a baptism in the way we understand baptism (an outward expression of the process of salvation). While our baptismal services follow the same pattern, John's baptism was actually a Jewish mikvah. A mikvah is for spiritual purification and consecration. It is a rite of passage to an elevated state of spirituality. As such, those who came to John the Baptist were preparing for the elevated state of spirituality that Messiah would bring.

A Jewish mikvah is always done by immersion. The reason is that, while immersed in water, you are placed within a totally different environment that you are accustomed. Immersion takes you out of the air and places you completely in water. Here you float aimlessly completely enveloped into the water. Your breathing cannot continue so you hold your breath. In a sense, you die. When you emerge from the gagging water, you breathe anew, symbolizing a newness of life.

When Yeshua came to be baptized of John, John protested. He insisted that he should be baptized by Yeshua! However, Yeshua told him to permit Him to be baptized and John did baptize him.

The reason Yeshua was baptized was because He was about to enter an elevated state of spirituality. Prior to this time, Yeshua had grown in favor with God and man. Now He was to enter into His ministry for God to man. It was a transition. To mark this transition, Yeshua went to the mikvah to be baptized by John.

When Elijah and Elisha reach the Jordan, they are both going to have a transition to a higher level of spirituality. One will be taken into heaven, the other will catch the mantle (with tzitzit attached) and receive the double portion. But the Jordan stands in the way.

The river Jordan had parted for the Israelites when the Ark of the Covenant (which represented the presence of God) first entered the Jordan when the priests that carried it stepped in. Now Elijah takes his mantle (which represents the presence of God that Elijah felt on Mount Horeb) and strikes the water of Jordan. The waters part and Elijah and Elisha walk through on dry land.

However, before Elisha can cross through Jordan he must first decide if he really wants to do this. Jordan represents separation. Once he follows Elijah to the other side and the waters flow back into a flowing river, all relationships will be forever altered. He will be different and as such will not fit in with his peers. He will have taken a step toward promotion and with that promotion comes responsibility. The step into Jordan is a step into a life that has higher standards to uphold than he has had heretofore.

However, the desire for the mantle with the double portion is great. Think of the lives that can be changed once he has the mantle. Think of the healings, deliverances, and most of all the revival of his beloved Israel with the eradication of Jezebel and her prophets of Baal.

Elisha does not hesitate. He follows Elijah through Jordan to the other side. Now the testing is complete. Elisha has passed every test with flying colors. Now comes the reward for his dedication.

Elijah said to Elisha, "Ask what I shall do for you before I am taken from you." Elisha then asked for a double portion. Elijah says that he has asked a hard thing.

It was a hard thing because the responsibility of the mantle would be great. The mantle makes you a target. The mantle means that you will be responsible for all those hundreds of students at all the schools of the prophets. The mantle means that Jezebel and Ahab will be your sworn enemies.

It was a hard thing because the mantle is a commission. There is a difference between a commission and a calling. A commission means that you are going to war. Elisha was called when the mantle was placed the first time in the field. Now he is receiving a commission on this second time anointing.

It is also a hard thing because it is not Elijah's to give. The double portion can only come from God.

Nevertheless, Elijah says to Elisha, "If you see me go, it shall happen for you". In other words, "If God sees fit to allow you to be with me when He takes me, I am sure God will grant you your request."

150

Sure enough, Elisha was there. The chariot of fire came and separated them and took Elijah into a whirlwind and then he was gone. As he was watching Elijah ascend, the mantle (with tzitzit attached) of Elijah came floating to the ground. Elisha picks up the mantle (with tzitzit attached), tears his own mantle in two pieces, walks over to the bank of the Jordan and says "Where is the God of Elijah?" and smites the water with the mantle.

When Elijah was taken up into heaven by a chariot of fire he passed his mantle to Elisha. Elijah did not die therefore his Tallit was not made ineffective but was instead passed on.

Our Elijah (Yeshua) was taken into heaven. Before He left, he told his disciples to go and wait in Jerusalem until they are "endued with power from on High" (Luke 24:49). The word "endued" is a Greek word that means "to be clothed upon". Yeshua's disciples were to wait in Jerusalem until they received something that would clothe them.

In Acts 2, "When the day of Pentecost fully came", the disciples in obedience to Yeshua were in the upper room in Jerusalem. Then "suddenly" there was a sound of a mighty wind and they were all filled with the Holy Ghost and they spoke with tongues as the Spirit gave them the words to speak.

On that eventful day in the upper room, the mantle of the Holy Spirit that was on Yeshua came floating down and clothed the disciples that were in the upper room. Now there would be a "double portion" for everyone who would receive this mantle.

Yeshua had said that we would do greater things than He did because He went to the Father. Just as Elisha did greater miracles than Elijah, so we will do greater miracles than Yeshua. How can that be? The only answer is that the same Spirit that was on Yeshua is now upon us.

As we embrace that fact we will be able to yield to the Holy Spirit and allow Him to do those "greater works" through us. We must shake off the feelings of inadequacy and renounce that lie. Yeshua Himself said we would do "greater works". We should simply believe Him.

Just as Elisha had to go and pick up the mantle, so we must pick up the mantle. In Acts chapter 3 we see Peter and John taking the mantle and using it to heal the lame man at the gate Beautiful (the Eastern Gate). This was the first miracle of the church and it mirrors the time when Elisha took the mantle of Elijah and smote the Jordan river.

Peter and John were on their way to the temple to pray (probably with their tallits over their shoulders). The lame man at the Eastern Gate (the Gate Beautiful) asked for alms (a gift that was a fulfillment of a commandment (mitzvah) that showed the righteousness of the person giving the gift). Peter, says to him, "look on us". Peter takes him by the hand and says to him, "In the name of Yeshua HaMaschiach (Jesus Christ) of Nazareth, rise up and walk". Peter then pulls the man to his feet and the man was healed and began walking and leaping and praising God!

By putting his faith in the name of Yeshua HaMaschiach, Peter caused that man to be healed. The Holy Spirit gave him the boldness to act in accordance to the power that was upon him through the mantle that was on him. He then preached the risen Christ. Since the miracles of Yeshua was still being done in His name, then that was proof that Yeshua was alive!

The mantle does us little good if we do not pick it up and say "Where is the God of Elijah?" Acts 1:8 quotes Yeshua as saying, *"Ye shall receive power after that the Holy Ghost is come upon you: and ye shall be witnesses..."*. Most of us do not have any problem with the witness part. We are expected to be a witness for Yeshua. But today we have a hard time with the power part of what Yeshua said. Today's churches are, in most places, a place of praise and prayer and purification but they have lost the ability to tap into God's power.

The life of a Christian (if God really exists) should be more than piety, worship, and devotion. For these things, any religion can offer. However, to be an extension of God in this earth through His ability, His knowledge, and His voice is an expression of life known only to those who are born of God's seed. The Christian alone can boast of a God inside. Comprehending what this means would revolutionize our influence on this earth.

152

Thank God that through the baptism of the Holy Ghost we enter through the door that brings God's power to our very fingertips, His knowledge is within our grasp, His voice is upon our lips.

Yes, Yeshua said, *"Ye shall receive power"* and power we have received through the nine gifts listed in I Corinthians 12:8-10. And these have enabled us to be witnesses not only of who Christ was and did, but also of who Christ is and is doing, and who Christ will always be and will be doing. Not just witnesses of past events, but of present and future events as revealed and performed by the Spirit of God.

The same God who worked miracles in the Old Testament by the prophets and by His Son while He was on the earth, is in these last days working with power by His Spirit through all that are open to His Spirit. Will you yield yourself to this double anointing?

There is one more interesting part to this story of Elijah and Elisha. It is taught by Jewish Rabbis throughout history that Elijah's mantle is still available. They believe that since Elisha did not pass the mantle that he received from Elijah to another, that the mantle was kept in store until Elijah would come just prior to Messiah's return. They look for Elijah every year at Passover. They believe they will recognize Elijah because of this mantle.

It is believed that at one time the mantle of Elijah was stored within the Altar of Incense. Now, think with me a little bit. Zacharias (who became John the Baptist's father) was doing the priestly service at the Altar of Incense when the angel appeared to him and told him he and his wife would have a son. Later in John the Baptist's ministry, some would wonder if he was Elijah. Although John denied it, Yeshua indicated that, if we would receive it, John was Elijah (at least in the spirit of Elijah). Could it be that the angel took the mantle of Elijah that was stored there and gave it to Zachariah to give to his son when he was old enough to receive it? Could it be that the people and the leaders recognized something about that mantle that made them think that John the Baptist was Elijah? It certainly is something to think about.

I would like to close this chapter with an invitation for you to receive this wonderful baptism in the Holy Spirit. There are those who are waiting for you to be "clothed with power from on High". There is a hurting and dying world out there that needs the power of God to break the yoke that has them in bondage.

Perhaps you have been filled with the Holy Spirit but you have not exercised His Presence in your life. I have good news, there is "fresh oil" waiting for you.

In either case, it is simple to receive the "double portion". You receive it exactly the same way Elisha received his double portion, you ask for it. Would you do so right now?

Chapter Ten
The Key of David

The prayer shawl is a portable Tabernacle where every individual may enter their own personal Holy of Holies to meet with God at the Mercy Seat. This is especially seen in the construction of the Tabernacle of David. However, the Tabernacle of David would never have been built without the key of David. In fact, it was the key of David that brought to us the understanding of the Melchizadek priesthood. We shall see how this all ties together in this chapter.

Isaiah 22:22 *"The key of the house of David I will lay on his shoulder; so he shall open, and no one shall shut; and he shall shut, and no one shall open."*

Revelation 3:7 *"And to the angel of the church in Philadelphia write, "These things says He who is holy, He who is true, "He who has the key of David, He who opens and no one shuts, and shuts and no one opens."*

These are the only two direct mentions of the key of David in the Bible. There are other indirect mentions that relate to the key of David and we will look at them as we delve into this study.

It is obvious that the key mentioned in these two verses is not an actual key in the material sense. The key of David is a spiritual key that has the ability to open and shut. We are immediately reminded of the keys of the kingdom that Yeshua spoke of in Matthew 16:15-19. The keys of the kingdom and the key of David are interrelated to each other.

A key represents authority and free access. A key implies permission to enter that which may have been locked and sealed up until now. Therefore, a key speaks of revelation and spiritual understanding.

Notice, however, it is called the key of David. Even when Yeshua speaks of this key, He does not call it His key. He still refers to it as the key of David.

So, what is the revelation of David and how does that apply to us today? We will begin to discover the answer to those questions and more as we continue to look into the Word of God.

Acts 13:22 (Amplified Bible, Classic Edition (AMPC) "And when He had deposed him, He raised up David to be their king; of him He bore witness and said, I have found David son of Jesse a man after My own heart, who will do all My will and carry out My program fully."

It is interesting that Paul (who was speaking here in this passage) called David "a man after God's own heart". Nothing is said about him being a great king or even a giant-killer. It seems that Paul considered David's greatest legacy was his propensity to seek the heart of God. This yearning for the heart of God caused David to "do all His will and carry out His program fully". In order to fully understand the "key of David," we will have to look at how David demonstrated the qualities that Paul has just described.

There are several unique things about David. Here are a few:

- Yeshua is said to be both David's "root and offspring" (Revelation 22:16). As a tree gets its sap from the roots, so David tapped into an "underground part" of himself and drew his strength. No other person is noted as having Yeshua as his root.

- David was the sole owner of a key. It is interesting that the key was not mentioned in the chronicles of his life. We don't see this key until God gives it to Eliakim (Isaiah 22:22). Even though the key was given to Eliakim, it was not his key. That key belonged to David. The key was David's revelation and spiritual understanding to unlock the worship of Heaven into his Tabernacle (or tent). When the days of David's Tabernacle was finished, this same worship was locked back up into the heavens for 1,000 years. This worship was unlocked again with the New Testament saints with the promise that God was raising up again the Tabernacle of David (Acts 15). When Yeshua proclaimed that He had the Key of David, He was signifying that what David had opened with that key He would be opening in the church age.

- He was unique in his understanding of Melchizadek (Hebrews 5-7). Before Yeshua came to earth to live, He came in the person of Melchizadek to pave the way for a king/priest on the very site where the Tabernacle would be raised (Psalms 76:1-2).

159

Melchizadek was King of Salem (the former name of Jerusalem). After Melchizadek's encounter with Abraham, no one even makes reference to Melchizadek except David. No one but David needed a revelation about Melchizadek. But David, in order to become a prototype of a New Testament paradigm, had to understand how to operate as a king/priest at the same time. He proclaims in Psalms 110 his revelation that the coming Messiah would be a priest forever after the order of Melchizadek. Before David, it was unlawful for any Old Testament saint, including a king, to enter into a priestly role.

- Also unique to David was his drive to possess Mount Zion as his capital. Hebron was a fine place for a capital, but David knew that he would not be able to "carry out God's plan fully" in Hebron. David knew that he must acquire Melchizadek's old hill. Israel had never been able to permanently possess it over the centuries of being in the promise land. But when God was ready for it, David was able to take the hill against all odds.

The question remains how David knew that it was permissible for him to not only build a Tabernacle but also to enter the priesthood, all the while still being a king. There was already a Tabernacle not far from the place where David was to erect his Tabernacle. The Tabernacle of Moses had been constructed through instructions directly from Heaven itself! How could David be so audacious to attempt to improve upon that?

The answer to these questions may come as we look at the events that led up to the building of the Tabernacle of David. The following will be necessarily brief and sketchy in order to stay within the confines of the subject matter of this book. However, I encourage you to read these stories in First Samuel and Second Samuel. You will be intrigued and blessed all at the same time.

The Tabernacle of Moses was at Shiloh. Eli was High Priest. Eli's two sons, Hophni, and Phinehas were vile men and Eli would not reprove them. Samuel was born and brought to Eli by Hannah who "lent him to the Lord as long as he lived". Samuel, as a young boy,

160

prophesies about the destruction of Eli's house. Samuel later becomes a Judge and a Prophet in Israel.

The Philistines had come out against Israel to fight and Israel began to lose the battle. The people called for the Ark of the Covenant to be brought out to see if it would help them. Hophni and Phinehas got the Ark out of the Holy of Holies and took it to the army.

This was in direct violation of several laws concerning the Ark of the Covenant. Among these would have been that only the High Priest (Eli) could enter the Holy of Holies and then only on the Day of Atonement after a series of purifications. Also, The Ark would have had to be covered in a prescribed manner. But this was war, and Hophni and Phinehas did not have time for such formalities. Nor did they care!

The result was that the battle was lost, the Ark of the Covenant was taken, and Hophni and Phinehas were killed. When Eli heard about the Ark of the Covenant being taken, he fell over backward and died. Also, Phinehas' wife died in childbirth when she heard about the Ark being taken. Her son was named Ichabod, which means "the glory has departed".

The Ark of the Covenant was taken by the Philistines and they suffered hemorrhoids in every city that the Ark was delivered. Finally, they determine to send the Ark back to Israel. They loaded the ark on a cart with two milk cows and sent it to Bethshemesh.

At Bethshemesh, some people looked into the Ark and thousands died. They then sent to Kirjath-jearim and asked them to come get the Ark. The Ark stayed at Kirjath-jearim all through the years of Samuel and also all through the years of King Saul.

So, the Ark remained at Kirjath-jearim until after David was crowned king of Judah and Israel. Once David had consolidated the kingdom, he took Jerusalem from the Jebusites and established Jerusalem as the capital. Now David begins to return the Ark of the Covenant back to the center of Israel's worship.

God has been working behind the scenes all the while, orchestrating events to fit within a long-range plan. Before He destroyed Eli's family and priesthood, He had Samuel brought to be trained by Eli and by His Holy Spirit. Eli did not realize it, but his replacement was growing up right under his nose.

Later this same Samuel would not only anoint the first king of Israel but also would anoint King David who would go get the Ark and put it in Jerusalem, the old city of Melchizadek (who was Yeshua in a pre-existent form).

Jerusalem (where Mount Zion is located) is known as the City of the Great King (Psalms 48:2). Jerusalem is not only an earthly city, but Heaven itself has a city called the new Jerusalem (Revelation 21:2). In fact, the Hebrew for Jerusalem is ירושלים (Yerushalayim, pronounced Yah-roo'-shah-lie-eem). The "im (ים)" suffix to a word makes the word plural in Hebrew. So it is seen that Jerusalem is the plural form meaning more than one. Therefore, we have a heavenly Jerusalem and an earthly Jerusalem.

So, we see that Jerusalem is more important to God than we may have ever thought. Jerusalem is the place where God chose to place His name (Deuteronomy 12:5; I Kings 9:3; II Chronicles 6:6; Nehemiah 1:9; Psalms 132:13; Zechariah 1:7 Zechariah 2:12; Zechariah 3:2).

Now David is bringing the Ark of the Covenant into Jerusalem. But David must learn a valuable lesson. In his exuberance to bring in the Ark, he does not carry the Ark as God instructed Moses. Instead, he puts it on a new cart. The oxen stumbled and Uzzah dies trying to keep the Ark from falling.

David stops the procession and puts the Ark in the house of Obed-Edom. For three months the Ark remains here. During these three months, David seeks the Lord about the proper way to bring back the Ark.

In just three short months, David not only knows how to bring back the Ark, but he also has plans for a tent to house the Ark, a large number of worshippers, a hosts of priests and recorders, as well as an understanding of himself as a king/priest after the order of Melchizadek. There is absolutely no way that David could have come up with all of this on his own. He must have had a download from Heaven to develop all of these plans. He had a revelation from God.

During this time, he was given a key to open the heavens and connect earthly Jerusalem with heavenly Jerusalem. This key would open the way for heavenly praise to connect to earth. This key would open the way to a new priesthood. This would be a priesthood of kings/priests, not after the order of Aaron but after the order of Melchizadek. David would be the connection between his root (Melchizadek) and his offspring (Yeshua), who are one and the same person.

David's Tabernacle was established to have worship around the Ark of the Covenant 24 hours a day. David would imitate, as much as possible, the worship that was happening in Heaven. Since worship never stops in Heaven, David made sure that worship would never stop in his Tabernacle.

(It is outside the scope of this book to look into the different aspects of David's Tabernacle. If the reader would like a great source of information on this subject, the author recommends the book by Kevin J. Conner, *The Tabernacle of David*.)

In the New Testament, we have a further revelation concerning the Tabernacle of David. In Acts 15 we find the growing church faced with a dilemma. Because of the ministry of Peter and Paul, the Gentiles were becoming followers of Yeshua the Messiah. There were some who thought that the Gentiles needed to become circumcised (which was a way to say that they needed to convert to Judaism). In other words, these people wanted the Gentiles to be Jewish Christians, not Gentile Christians. The church was in danger of becoming two separate groups, a Gentile church, and a Jewish church.

James (the pastor of the church and half-brother of Yeshua) after hearing Peter and Paul made this announcement concerning the Gentiles.

Acts 15:13-21 *"And after they had become silent, James answered, saying, "Men and brethren, listen to me: Simon has declared how God at the first visited the Gentiles to take out of them a people for His name. And with this the words of the prophets agree, just as it is written:*

After this I will return and will rebuild the tabernacle of David, which has fallen down; I will rebuild its ruins, and I will set it up; so that the rest of mankind may seek the LORD, even all the Gentiles who are called by My name, says the LORD who does all these things.

Known to God from eternity are all His works. Therefore, I judge that we should not trouble those from among the Gentiles who are turning to God, but that we write to them to abstain from things polluted by idols, from sexual immorality, from things strangled, and from blood. For Moses has had throughout many generations those who preach him in every city, being read in the synagogues every Sabbath."

James connects the Tabernacle of David with the coming in of the Gentiles. Back in Matthew 16:19, Yeshua gave to Peter the keys of the kingdom to bind, loose, open, and shut. It was Peter on the Day of Pentecost who used this key to open the understanding of the Jewish people. Then again, at Cornelius house, it was Peter who opened the way for the Gentiles to receive the same experience that the Jewish people received on the Day of Pentecost.

James sees this as a fulfillment of Joel's prophecy of the Tabernacle of David being rebuilt. First of all, the Jewish people came under this tent when the mantle of the Holy Spirit fell on them. Then the Gentiles received this same mantle and they also came under this tent. James saw both Jew and Gentile worshipping together under one tent! There was no wall of separation.

Therefore, we see that James saw the Tabernacle of David as a tent where both Jews and Gentiles would be in unity. This unity is what is being referred to in Psalms 133:1-3

"Behold, how good and how pleasant it is for brethren to dwell together in unity! It is like the precious oil upon the head, running down on the beard, the beard of Aaron, running down on the edge of his garments. It is like the dew of Hermon, descending upon the mountains of Zion; for there the LORD commanded the blessing — life forevermore."

Christians, traditionally, have looked at this Psalm as meaning a coming together of the different sects of Christianity, but this could not be farther from the truth. That kind of coming together is ecumenicalism and is demonic.

Unity comes from coming under the same tent, as in the Tabernacle of David. Since we have connected this tent with the baptism of the Holy Spirit, that both Jews and Gentiles received, the only unity that we should seek is the *"unity of the Spirit in the bond of peace"* (Ephesians 4:3-6).

Only when we come to the place where we have accepted *"one Lord, one faith, one baptism, one God and Father of all"* can we have unity. I Corinthians 12:13-14 says *"For by one Spirit we were all baptized into one body – whether Jews or Greeks, whether slaves or free – and have all been made to drink into one Spirit."*

So we see that Jews and Gentiles are unified through salvation (being "baptized into one body") and the baptism of the Holy Spirit (being "made to drink into one Spirit"). Two separate acts.

It was when Jews and Gentiles both were born again and subsequently received the baptism of the Holy Spirit, evidenced by them speaking in other tongues, did we see the middle wall of partition broken. It was the relationship to the Holy Spirit that made the difference. It is the Holy Spirit upon Jew and Gentile that will unify us into one body – the "one new man" (Ephesians 2:14-15).

This is the Key of David and is represented by the prayer shawl. When we wear the prayer shawl, we are wearing a prophetic statement about Davidic worship being restored with Jews and Gentiles under one banner (one miracle mantle)

As long as Jews and Gentiles worshiped in unity together there were great miracles in the church. However, there was also great persecution. This persecution continued until Emperor Constantine made Christianity the official religion of the Roman Empire in 313 A.D. The persecution stopped but at great cost to the presence of the Holy Spirit and miracles.

Soon the Roman Catholic Church was begun and anti-Semitism pushed the Jewish community out of the church. We built back the wall of separation and fortified it with the Crusades and the Holocaust. Now we have a wall that makes it extremely hard for

Jewish people to become Christians. We should work hard to tear down that wall.

One of the ways we can begin to tear down that wall is to learn of our Hebraic roots. The prayer shawl is an excellent starting point. The prayer shawl is the key of David laid upon our shoulders that unlocks the barrier between Jew and Gentile. While we are not required to become Jewish or to come under the law, we would benefit greatly by understanding the teaching that the prayer shawl provides. This understanding would give us a tool to speak to the Jewish people about the richness that is in Yeshua. It would help to bridge the gap between Jew and Gentile.

The prayer shawl is the key of David that is laid upon our shoulders. With the white that signifies priesthood and the tekhelet (blue) that signifies kingship, we are reminded that we are kings and priests unto God (Revelation 1:6). The prayer shawl represents the Melchizadek priesthood of the king/priest.

Not only does the prayer shawl (which is the key of David laid on our shoulders) reveal to us the Melchizadek priesthood, but also it teaches us about the Holy Spirit which "clothed us with power from on high". When we put on the prayer shawl we are reminded of the Holy Spirit that envelops our life. We are anointed by Him for service. It is the miracle mantle from Yeshua to do the works that He did and greater works.

The prayer shawl is a personal tent where we can enter into our own personal Holy of Holies and worship around the Ark of the Covenant any time of the day. In this tent of the Holy Spirit, we can receive revelation knowledge through the gifts of the Spirit (I Corinthians 12). In this tent, we will pray with the Spirit and we will pray with the understanding also. We will sing in the Spirit and we will sing with the understanding also (I Corinthians 14:15). In this tent, Heaven is brought to earth.

Chapter Eleven
Marriage

Ezekiel 16:8-14 *"When I passed by you again and looked upon you, indeed your time was the time of love; so I spread My wing over you and covered your nakedness. Yes, I swore an oath to you and entered into a covenant with you, and you became Mine," says the Lord GOD. "Then I washed you in water; yes, I thoroughly washed off your blood, and I anointed you with oil. I clothed you in embroidered cloth and gave you sandals of badger skin; I clothed you with fine linen and covered you with silk. I adorned you with ornaments, put bracelets on your wrists, and a chain on your neck. And I put a jewel in your nose, earrings in your ears, and a beautiful crown on your head. Thus you were adorned with gold and silver, and your clothing was of fine linen, silk, and embroidered cloth. You ate pastry of fine flour, honey, and oil. You were exceedingly beautiful, and succeeded to royalty. Your fame went out among the nations because of your beauty, for it was perfect through My splendor which I had bestowed on you," says the Lord GOD."*

This Scripture describes beautifully the love that God has for his bride. The entire Bible is a story of how God wanted a bride who would be his wife. Pictures of weddings are all through the Bible beginning in Genesis with Adam and Eve and culminating with the Marriage Supper of the Lamb.

Through the pages, God is wooing, courting, promising, and ultimately sacrificing Himself all in an effort to demonstrate His love for us and to win us as His bride. Unfortunately, we have made it difficult for Him to convince us of His love. Not only that but, like Israel, we have had our "other lovers". Instead of embracing the love of our Divine suitor, we have trusted in uncertain riches, elusive promotions, worldly power, sexual satisfaction, or a host of other imposters vying for our devotion. Even worry and fear have asked for our hand in marriage and we have accepted, all too eagerly.

Though we may have initially accepted His proposal, we have become an unfaithful spouse. Instead of trusting and leaning on His wonderful arm, we instead lean on the arm of flesh. As Isaiah as said, "Who has believed our report and to whom is the arm of the Lord revealed?" The answer to this is that the "arm of the Lord" is revealed to those who "believed our report". What is this report? It is all through the Bible! God loves you! God wants to take you "under His wing"! God wants you to be His very own. God wants to care for you, love you, provide for you, be your closest friend. God wants to be your Husband.

The phrase "so I spread my wing over you" in the above verse is a direct reference to a Biblical proposal of marriage. "Wing", in this verse, is the word for the corner of a garment. God is using the mental image of Himself spreading the corner of His tallit over his people in a proposal of marriage.

The phrase "I swore an oath to you and entered a covenant with you" signifies the giving of the Ketubah and the acceptance of the bride price. From this point on God and Israel were betrothed. Israel became His possession.

The phrase "I washed you with water" refers to the mikvah (baptism) that the bride and groom would perform prior to the final wedding (Nisuin). There is also a reference to their being a king and queen on their wedding day when it speaks of "a beautiful crown on your head". The rest of the verse describes the gifts that God gives to His beloved to help her become His beautiful bride without spot or wrinkle.

In this chapter, we are going to look at many of the Biblical references to a wedding and put together what great lengths God has gone in order to win you as His bride. It is my hope that this will get deep into your sub-conscious so that you will never doubt His love for you ever again. Your faith will soar. Your trust will be unbounded. Your confidence will never be shaken. It is my prayer, like Paul said in Ephesians, *"that you may know what is the hope of His calling, what are the riches of the glory of His inheritance in the saints, and what is the exceeding greatness of His power toward us who believe…"*

Jewish weddings in Bible times were dramatically different than weddings in today's world. Although modern Jewish weddings still maintain some of the traditions we find in the Biblical text, in the main they are quite removed from their ancient counterparts.

The first step for marriage is called the Shiddukhin (שִׁדּוּכִין pronounced shid-doo'-keen). This began what may have been a very long process. the process was initiated by the father of the prospective groom or by his representative. Once a favorable girl was deemed worthy, the father of the groom (or his representative) would then set up a meeting with the father of the prospective bride.

Two Biblical examples of Shiddukhin are the selecting of a bride for Isaac and the story of Samson and a Philistine woman. In the first example, Eliezer had met Rebekah at a well. After determining that "this is the one", he then requests to go to her house to meet her father. In the latter example, Samson had met a woman whom he really liked and then asked his father and mother to arrange a meeting for the purpose of getting her for his wife.

The next step in the marriage process would consist of the son's father or the young man himself going to the house of the bride-to-be with a flask of wine. They would inquire concerning the price of the bride called the Mohar (מהר pronounced moh'-her). The Mohar is set by the girl's father and reflects the value that he places on her. Initially, this was to reimburse the girl's father for the cost of raising her for her future husband.

If the Mohar is agreed upon by both parties, the girl is called in and they all drink wine together. If the girl drinks the wine, she is showing her willingness to become the young man's wife.

A temporary contract is drawn up called a tenaim (תנאים pronounced tuh-nah'-im). This is basically a promise to be married at a future time. It will include the amount of the Mohar, the rights of the bride, and any promises that are made. This will form the basis for a subsequent permanent document called the Ketubah (כתובה pronounced keh-too'-bah).

The writing of the Ketubah would occur many days later. The Bride would "count the days" until the Ketubah was written. So there is a direct connection between the paying of the Mohar and the writing of the Ketubah.

There is a "counting of the days" between Pesach and Shavuot. The Jewish people call this "the counting of the omer". By doing so, they connect Shavuot (Pentecost) with Pesach (Passover).

Both events are essential. Pesach (Passover) delivers them from Egypt. Shavuot (Pentecost) gives them authority as a nation. From a Christian perspective, Pesach (Passover) is our freedom from satan's dominion and Shavuot (Pentecost) is our empowerment with the anointing and authority of Holy Spirit.

From this point on the couple are betrothed to each other. Betrothal in Hebrew is Eyrusin (אירוסין pronounced ear'-u-sin). This is referred to as the Kiddushin (קידושין pronounced kid'-doo-shin), which means sanctification or setting apart. They are considered husband and wife even though they will not live with each other or have sexual relations.

The record of Mary (her Hebrew name is Miriam) and Joseph (his Hebrew name is Yosef) show this relationship. The term espouse means betrothal. This relationship is binding and the couple, even though not fully married, would have to get a divorce to break it. This is what is meant by Yosef going to put away (divorce) Miriam privately.

At this point, the young man would say, *"In my Father's house are many rooms, I am going to prepare a place for you. I will come again and receive you unto myself that where I am, there you will be also."* She belongs to him now for she has been "bought with a price" (Mohar). This does not mean property, in the sense of other material goods, for he could never sell her, even partially. They "belonged" to each other. This is best expressed in Song of Solomon 6:3, *"I am my beloved's and He is mine"*.

The young man goes to prepare a chamber in his father's house. This is referred to in Hebrew as a Chuppah (חפה pronounced, koo-pah'). In modern times, this has evolved to a covering over the couple at the wedding held by 4 poles. Even today this still represents the room, or honeymoon suite, where the couple would normally have spent their first week together as man and wife.

The Hebrew letters for Chuppah, when viewed individually and put into a sentence, tells a story, so to speak, of what a Chuppah is and does. Since Hebrew is written from right to left, we will look at the letter at the far right of the word (for us English speaking people this is reading backward).

The first letter is ח and is pronounced "Chet" (ch as in Bach). This letter is a picture of a fence in Paleo-Hebrew and, among other things, represents a closed inner chamber.

The second letter is פ *and (because it has a dot in the center of the letter) is pronounced "Peh" (without the dot in the center it would be and "F" sound). This second letter is a picture of a mouth and represents speaking.*

The last letter is ה and is pronounced "Hay". Although it looks similar to the Chet, you will notice it has a small opening on the left side of the letter. This opening is an open window and shows openness and freedom.

Therefore, when we put the definitions of each of these letters together we arrive at the following description of a Chuppah. ***"A closed inner chamber where you can speak openly and freely".***

Now, since the Chuppah is where the couple would consummate their marriage, it is easy to see that this would correspond with the inner chamber of our home (the bedroom). It is the place of intimacy. It is the most sacred part of our home. Couples can be open and free with each other. Inhibitions are cast aside. (I am going into detail because I want us to see a spiritual aspect.) The Prayer Shawl (tallit) is our own personal Chuppah where we can lock the door and commune openly and freely in this holy inner chamber with our Savior and Lord, the lover of our soul.

Yeshua told His disciples *"…when you pray, go into your room, and when you have shut your door, pray to your Father who is in the secret place; and your Father who sees in secret will reward you openly."* (Matthew 6:6). Yeshua was speaking directly about the prayer shawl that every Jewish man would pray under. The "secret place" refers directly to Psalms 91 where it talks about the "secret place of the Most High".

Here under the Prayer Shawl, you can have an uninhibited relationship with the God of the Universe. You can ask whatever you want, talk about whatever you want, sing, and dance, and laugh, and cry. You can be serious or light-hearted. No one cares! You are with Him!

During the time that the young man is preparing the Chuppah, the girl will spend her time learning how to be a wife and mother, and to learn how to please her husband.

If the young man is asked when the day of the wedding will be, he will say, *"No man knows the day or the hour, only my Father"*. It is a personal thing for him, and he will only talk about the time of his coming with his father.

This statement is also a catch-phrase for the Feast of Trumpets (Yom Teruah תרוצה יום pronounced yom teh-ru'-ah). Today it is referred to a Rosh HaShanah (pronounced rosh ha-shah-nah') (the head of the year). This is over a 2-day period because no one can be absolutely certain when it begins. Everyone listens for the "last shofar" (trump).

Both the bride and the groom will go to a Mikvah (מקווה pronounced mik'-vah) for ceremonial cleansing prior to the wedding. The Mikvah is what our Baptismal ceremony is modeled after. They immerse three times, saying a blessing each time. (Most Christian baptisms are done in the Name of the Father, and of the Son, and of The Holy Spirit – three names, one baptism.)

Yeshua, our groom was baptized in the Jordan River. John's baptism was a Mikvah for teshuva (תשובה pronounced teh-shoo-vah'). Teshuva is translated repentance, but its meaning is "to turn". John's baptism was to ceremonially cleanse those who came, in preparation for the Messiah. The baptismal candidate would have to show fruits of their turning toward the coming Messiah before John would baptize them in the Mikvah.

This baptism differs from Christian baptism in that the Christian purpose is to identify with the death, burial, and resurrection of our Lord and Savior. Christian baptism is a personal identification of a past event. The Mikvah baptism of John was a preparation for a future event.

175

At first, John did not want to baptize Yeshua. However, Yeshua insisted that John baptize Him in "order to fulfill all righteousness". Yeshua was doing what was necessary in order to become our Husband. We follow Him in baptism because we want to show that we belong to Him because He paid the Mohar (the price for our union with Him).

The groom sends gifts to his betrothed. These gifts are called the Matan (מתן pronounced mah-tahn'). The Matan (means Bridal gift) is his pledge, to his betrothed, of his love for her, that he was thinking of her, and that he would return to receive her as his wife.

Yeshua gave us the Holy Spirit as well as the gifts of the Holy Spirit as a Matan. Ephesians 1:14 says that the Holy Spirit is *the earnest of our inheritance until the redemption of the purchased possession*. "Earnest", is the down payment (or guarantee) that Yeshua will come and receive what He has purchased through the Mohar. He also gave us eternal life (John 10:22-28), peace (John 14:27), and an open check that we could write for anything we needed (John 14:13-14). How awesome is our Groom, our Savior, our soon coming King!

When he comes for his bride, there is great fanfare. There is a shofar blast and someone says, "The Bridegroom is coming!" All of his friends, family, and servants come in a grand parade with music and rejoicing. He snatches his bride and carries her away to the place that He has prepared.

Then begins the wedding ceremony called the Nisuin (נשואין pronounced nigh'-soo-inn). The couple will fast on the day of their wedding because this day represents a personal Yom Kippur (כפור יום pronounced yahm kih-puhr') where their previous sins are forgiven. It is a start of a new beginning for their lives, no longer individuals, but one in marriage.

Yeshua made reference to this fasting in Matthew 9:15 *"Can the friends of the bridegroom mourn as long as the bridegroom is with them? But the days will come when the bridegroom will be taken away from them, and then they will fast."* One of the purposes of fasting is to demonstrate our longing for our betrothed Husband to come and get us to be with Him.

The wedding ceremony is conducted under a Chuppah. As stated earlier, this represents the place that the groom has prepared for the bride. It is a canopy held on four poles. This is also representative of Mount Sinai where God had a wedding rehearsal with Israel. The marriage was never fully consummated. Therefore, they remained in betrothal. The Hebrew actually says that the congregation of Israel came "under" the mountain to hear God speak. This was referring to them coming under the cloud that was covering the Mountain and enough surrounding area to overshadow the congregation as well. (Not, as the Jewish sages suggest, that God raised the Mountain over the heads of the Jewish people and they stood under the Mountain!).

The Groom enters the Chuppah and waits for his bride to meet him. We are told I Thessalonians 4:16-17 that we will meet Him in the clouds. The first part of those verses talk about Him coming for us (as I have described earlier). The last part of those verses identify us making the trip to His holy Chuppah that He has prepared where we will be with him forever. It is here "in the clouds" that we will be married. Up until this time, we were betrothed (espoused). Now, He has come for His purchased possession! Oh! How I long for that day!

Next, the Bride enters the Chuppah and immediately circles the Groom seven times. This has several interpretations. One interpretation is that she is building her house (As God built the first house for man in a seven-day creation). Another interpretation is that, like the city of Jericho, she is tearing down the walls of separation and creating openness and honesty in their marriage. More importantly, this is a symbol for the seven years we will be having the Marriage Supper of the Lamb.

Then four men will take a tallit (prayer shawl) and hold it over the couple. This signifies that the couple is under the "wings of God" and are under His protection and provision.

The Groom, who is wearing a tallit, puts his arm around her, symbolizing that she is now "under his wing" of protection and provision. This symbolizes a "double portion" given to the Bride. One portion from God, the other portion from her husband.

177

At Salvation, the Holy Spirit comes to dwell in us and that is made possible by Yeshua's blood and by asking Him to save us. Then, we get the 2nd infilling of the Holy Spirit when we are "clothed with power from on High". This is given to us by God Himself. Yeshua said in John 14:16-17, "*And I will pray the Father, and He will give you another Helper, that He may abide with you forever – the Spirit of truth, whom the world cannot receive, because it neither sees Him nor knows Him; but you know Him, for He dwells with you and will be in you.*"

God gives us the Holy Spirit "whom the world cannot receive". The world can receive the Holy Spirit that Yeshua gives, or none could be saved. This is the part of the Holy Spirit that can only come on those who have already been indwelt. He goes on to say that "He (the Holy Spirit) already dwells with you". Then He adds, "and will be in you". In other words, the Holy Spirit that dwells and abides will come a 2nd time and permeate your entire being. You will be baptized, immersed, overwhelmed with His Presence.

The two prayer shawls reflect this perfectly! Yeshua gives us the Holy Spirit that dwells with us (as depicted by the groom with the prayer shawl around us) and God the Father gives us the Holy Spirit that overshadows us and completely overwhelms us.

The Ketubah is then read out loud and handed to the Bride for her to keep. This stipulates the promises that the groom makes for the Bride as well as the Bride's price (Mohar), any gifts (Matan) that have been given to her, and the Bride's consent that is witnessed by two witnesses.

A cup of wine is poured and someone reads the Seven Blessings:

- Blessed are you, God, who brings forth fruit from the vine.
- Blessed are you, God, who shapes the universe. All things created speak of your glory.
- Blessed are you, Holy One, who fashions each person.
- We bless you, God, for forming each person in your image. You have planted within us a vision of you and given us the means that we may flourish through time. Blessed are you, Creator of humanity.

178

- May Israel, once bereft of her children, now delight as they gather together in joy. Blessed are you, God, who lets Zion rejoice with her children.
- Let these loving friends taste of the bliss you gave to the first man and woman in the Garden of Eden in the days of old. Blessed are you, the Presence who dwells with bride and groom in delight.
- Blessed are You, who lights the world with happiness and contentment, love and companionship, peace and friendship, bridegroom and bride. Let the mountains of Israel dance! Let the gates of Jerusalem ring with the sounds of joy, song, merriment, and delight — the voice of the groom and the voice of the bride, the happy shouts of their friends and companions. We bless you, God, who brings bride and groom together to rejoice in each other.

After these blessings are read, the couple will drink from the cup of wine. This is the final seal of the covenant of marriage and only one more part remains.

It is interesting that in Revelation Yeshua pronounced seven blessings over the seven churches at the end of each message that John was to give to them (Revelation 2:7, 11, 17, 2-28, 3:5, 12, 21). The imagery that John saw (the seven candlesticks with Yeshua standing in the middle of them, Revelation 1:12-13) would be a picture of the betrothed Bride of Christ. Each candlestick had seven branches totaling 49 branches. Adding Yeshua, in the center, as the 50th branch, you would have a direct reference to Shavuot (Pentecost) where the Ketubah (the Torah) was read and accepted 50 days after Pesach (Passover). This reinforces that the church (Jew and Gentile) are the betrothed Bride of Christ.

The Church (represented by seven candlesticks) is a picture of the Bride circling the groom (Yeshua) seven times. We are introduced to a wedding ceremony in the very first chapters of Revelation. Therefore, at least part of Revelation is a vision of our wonderful wedding with our Lord and Savior Yeshua HaMaschiach.

The couple will retire to a private room and close the door. There will be food and drink for them and they will break their fast. This is the first meal that they will have eaten together as husband and wife and they will do so in private. This is also symbolic of the ancient custom of the bride and groom staying for 7 days in their Bridal chamber (Chuppah). The friend of the groom stands guard outside the door making sure they are not disturbed. After about 15 minutes or so, they will emerge and join the party already in progress.

The wedded couple are treated as a King and a Queen. There are special chairs, like thrones, that they will sit in while everyone comes by to congratulate them. It is customary for them to be given crowns to wear.

The Nisuin part of the wedding has not yet been fulfilled, not with Israel nor with the Church. There are some who teach that Israel was made the Bride of God at Mount Sinai. God Himself said that He is her Husband. However, that is true only in the Betrothal sense of the word. Nowhere is it recorded where Israel entered into a private chamber to consummate the marriage. The only private chamber where God resided was the Holy of Holies and it was physically impossible for three million Jews to come into that relatively small space. In fact, only one Jew could come in and that was the High Priest. Even he could not come in except once a year and only as a representative, a go-between. While it is true that the tallit with its tzitzits represented a personal Holy of Holies, only one Jew at a time could enter into each tallit.

Israel remains a betrothed wife who has been divorced. As such, the Groom is free to woo her back to Him, if He desires. He can even become betrothed to her again and ultimately marry her in full Nisuin. If she was a wife in the fullest sense of the word, once divorced the Groom would be prohibited from marrying her again.

Deuteronomy 24:1-4 *"When a man takes a wife and marries her, and it happens that she finds no favor in his eyes because he has found some uncleanness in her, and he writes her a certificate of divorce, puts it in her hand, and sends her out of his house, when she has departed from his house, and goes and becomes another man's wife, if the latter husband detests her and writes her a certificate of divorce, puts it in her hand, and sends her out of his house, or if the latter husband dies who took her as his wife, then her former husband who divorced her must not take her back to be his wife after she has been defiled; for that is an abomination before the LORD, and you shall not bring sin on the land which the LORD your God is giving you as an inheritance."*

A "Get" (Bill of Divorce) that occurred only after the Betrothal marriage had different legalities than a "Get" occurring after Nisuin marriage. That Hebrew couple who had reached the second stage of Nisuin marriage and then divorced were not allowed by the Scriptures to marry each other again. The reason was that they had already engaged in marital relations (Deuteronomy 24:1-4). The Scripture says, "When a man hath taken a wife **AND** marries her". A husband is marrying his wife twice. He has already taken a wife in betrothal and now he is marrying her in full Nisuin marriage. So this prohibition only applies where the marriage has reached Nisuin and not Erusin (betrothal).

It was an ancient part of Jewish law based on these Torah verses that a couple only betrothed (meaning they haven't had marital relations nor lived together) could get divorced and eventually come back together again. In other words, Israel as a divorced betrothed bride could be betrothed to God again, if she repented and changed her ways and desired to be faithful to the marriage contract, the Torah, and God.

Yeshua came to Judah (still married to God, but unfaithful) in the first century pleading with the Jews to repent (to return to Torah/Marriage Contract) and enter the Kingdom of God. God had sent Yeshua to persuade the betrothed bride to return to Him. Collectively the Jewish nation had drifted far away from God and did not heed the call (Matthew 23:37-39).

Because there are two separate parts to a Jewish wedding, the Betrothal, and the Nisuin, there is a distinction between divorcing a Betrothed Bride and a Bride that is a full Bride through Nisuin.

Those that teach "Replacement Theology" hold that Israel was divorced by God (Jeremiah 3:8) and now it is impossible for God to marry Israel again (Deuteronomy 24:1-4). They teach that the Church has "replaced" Israel and the New Testament (covenant) is a Ketubah for the church.

Under their teaching, the only way for a Jewish person to come into the New Covenant (Ketubah) is for them to completely leave their Judaism with its feast days and Sabbaths to become a Christian within the Gentile Church. This is a reversal of the dilemma that faced the Early Church with the Gentiles being challenged by the Judaizers that they needed to be circumcised and become Jewish. This would include the Gentile believers coming under not only the Law of Moses but also the Oral Law.

The judgment of James the Pastor of the Jerusalem church, as well as being the half-brother of Yeshua, settled that for all time. We should learn from this and realize that not only are Gentiles not required to be Jewish to become Christians, neither should Jews be required to forsake their Jewishness to become a Christian.

We need to develop an understanding and tolerance of their culture as they also develop an understanding and tolerance of our culture. This would then pave the way for us becoming the One New Man spoken of in Ephesians 2:14-18. We would then realize, as James the Pastor of Jerusalem, that the Tabernacle of David which is fallen is being restored once again.

At this point, I would like to take what we have learned about Jewish Weddings to go through the Bible and show the extent that God has gone through in order to get a Bride for His Son. In order to understand the process, we will need to not only understand Jewish Weddings, we will need to understand Biblical Divorce in the context of the Jewish mindset.

Beginning with Adam and Eve, God has always desired a family. God is love (I John 4:8 and 4:16). This is who God is. Love is what defines God. While God loves the Son and the Son loves the Father, there is a desire within the Godhead to bestow their affection on someone else other than themselves. Love needs an object to pour its affection on. Therefore, God created man.

However, man must learn of the Creator's love. He will have to discover the love that God has for him. When Adam was created, he had not yet experienced God's love. Adam was created in God's image and likeness and was himself given a loving nature. God gave Adam a wife so that Adam would be able to understand to some degree what kind of love God had for him.

So, God created a woman and brought her to Adam and performed a wedding ceremony in the Garden. Eve would come to understand God's love from the manner of love that Adam showed to her. God would use the marriage of Adam and Eve to communicate His love. The concept of marriage would be a frequent picture that God would use to reveal His love to all mankind.

God had prepared all of the creation for His man. This was a grand gift of enormous proportions. Then, in a small parcel of ground, God prepared a Garden, just Eastward of Eden. This Garden was to be a Chuppah where God could be intimate with His man and woman. God covered them with glory, which would be like a garment over them. This glory is a spiritual tallit and as the tallit is a holy garment, so the glory over man was God's holiness and righteousness covering their total being.

God withheld nothing from man, except for the fruit from one tree. On a fateful day, Adam and Eve were exploring the Garden together and a serpent spoke and got Eve's attention. This serpent was another lover who sought to entice and lure God's creation into an adulterous relationship with himself.

Through a series of questions, the serpent was able to cause Eve to question God's love for her. Why would God withhold this tree? He gave us everything else. What is it about this tree that God doesn't want us to experience? Isn't it unfair of Him to place something here so close to us and then not allow us to enjoy it? I can see that it is good for food. It feels wonderful in my hand. I wonder if it tastes as good as it looks and feels. Why doesn't God love me enough to let me enjoy this fruit? Why doesn't God love me enough to allow me to know both good and evil? Doesn't He trust me?

So, Eve took of the fruit of the tree and ate it. Then she turns to her husband, Adam, who was there all the while with her, and offers him the fruit.

Adam knew immediately the consequence of eating of this tree. He knew that, while the tree yielded some temporary pleasure, the end result would be death. That is what God said. All that Adam knew about death, is it meant, "to not exist anymore". His only understanding would have been total annihilation. God made him, He certainly could unmake him. That was his perception of death.

Here is where an example of God's love is played out for all humanity to see. Adam, looked at Eve and his love for her became greater than his love for God and even his love for his own life. Adam could not bear to be without his bride. So, deliberately, and with full awareness of his decision, he took the fruit and ate it himself.

By that one act, without even realizing it, he made it possible for Eve to be saved. Because Adam chose to die and take on Eve's sin, Eve could bear children and eventually a Savior would be born that would redeem mankind. Eve would be saved in childbearing. It would be the "seed of woman" who would grow up into manhood and be the Last Adam and take on Eve's sin and nail it to a cross.

Adam's sacrifice for his wife typified Yeshua's sacrifice for the sins of the world. It also demonstrated the extent of love. It is love that makes a man lay down his life for another.

God comes into the Garden, the Divine Chuppah, in the cool of the day. He desires intimacy with his creation. Adam and Eve hear His voice in the Garden. Fear grips their hearts! This is the moment that they will cease to exist! God told them they would die and here He is to make good on His promise! So, they hid. Not so much to keep God from finding them, for they surely realized that God knew where they were. They hid so that they would delay the inevitable and at least enjoy some final moments together before they would be disintegrated.

But then, they hear something wonderful. God says, "Adam, where are you?" This isn't a God who wants to destroy them. They are not "sinners in the hands of an angry God". This is a God who is concerned about them. He wants to know where they are. He wants to be with them. In those words, there was communicated something beyond the gift of creation that He gave them. God was not just a Giver of gifts, He was a caring and compassionate lover.

Creation was nice, but it was material. This was something else! They had not felt this before. This was spiritual. This was tenderness. Something was coming out of God's heart. There was compassion in His voice. For the first time, they felt love from God.

It was from the depth of their sin that they found the extent of God's love. Though they were yet sinners, God still loved them.

So Adam and Eve came out of hiding. Adam says, "We were afraid because we were naked, we lost the glory (the Tallit) that you gave us. We tried to make it ourselves, but look, we didn't do a very good job."

Adam is avoiding the issue. Their nakedness was the result, not the cause. The loss of the glory was not, as Adam suggested, simply a misplacement of a garment.

God begins a series of questions to get to the bottom of the situation. Finally, they admit what they had done, trying to shift the blame as much as possible. God wants to fix the problem, but they must be honest in order for Him to be of any help. Before they got into this mess, God had a plan to get them out. God never expected them to do it on their own. He knew they needed His help.

The next thing God does is to let them know that they are not going to cease to exist, at least not in the immediate future. He says to Eve, "I will put hostility between the serpent's seed and your seed". This was very comforting to Eve. This meant that she would at least stay around long enough to have children! She was not going to disintegrate.

In addition, God was leaving behind a promise of a "seed of woman" who would ultimately bruise the head of the serpent. This tells us of a virgin-born Child who would grow up and defeat this old enemy and reverse the curse of death that came because of Eve's disobedience.

Oh, the love of God! Though they were worthy of annihilation, God made a way of escape for them. God so loved them that He made a way! God then showed them what it would take to renew their relationship with Him. He killed an animal and took the skins and made them a coat.

The word for "coat" is the very same Hebrew word that is used for Joseph's coat of many colors. God literally made for Adam and Eve a physical Tallit that they could wear to replace the spiritual Tallit (glory) that they had originally. By wearing this tallit, they would be reminded of the sacrifice of the animal that covered them. This would be a picture of a later sacrifice that would be made to not just cover them, but to completely remove their sin.

But they could not stay in His Chuppah. They had committed spiritual adultery. Although they did not have intimacy with God within the Chuppah, symbolizing the consummation of their marriage with God, they had been symbolically betrothed to God when they accepted His terms of living in the Garden. Therefore, God drove them out of the Garden. This is the equivalent of a divorce.

Nevertheless, God begins a long drawn out process of bringing His creation back to Him where He can have intimacy within the Chuppah. Children are born and relationships are made. A man by the name of Noah finds grace in the sight of the Lord. While all other men reject His offer of betrothal, one man says, "Yes". God says that He will begin with this man and his family and develop them into a people who would want to become His bride. The flood comes, and the process begins.

Later we find another man who will accept His proposal. Abraham will become a father of people who will know the love of God in a special way and will influence all those around them. Through this people, God will be able to show how much He loves His creation.

God, through the life of Abraham and his son Isaac, demonstrates his plan for returning His creation back to Him. God would demonstrate His love so dramatically and so unmistakably that His love would be strikingly evident to every man.

The getting of a bride for Isaac shows how God would send a representative (the Holy Spirit) to seek and to find a worthy bride and bring her back to His Son's house. The sacrifice of Isaac on the altar on Mount Moriah would show how God would give His only begotten Son to show the full extent of His love.

Isaac would have sons as well. One son, Jacob, would become the father of 12 sons. Those sons would be the fathers of the 12 tribes of Israel.

One of those 12 sons, Joseph, would be sold into Egypt. Joseph goes from a favored son, to a slave, then a prisoner, and then ultimately and suddenly rises to be the 2nd in command over the entire Egyptian Empire.

A famine would occur, Jacob and his 11 sons would eventually unite with their 12th brother, Joseph, who was already in Egypt. After many years, they would become slaves in Egypt.

In Egypt, the Israelites would multiply into a vast nation of people. Finally, since the time that He divorced Adam and Eve, God is ready to make His offer to this family of people. The question would be whether they would accept His proposal of marriage.

God needed a representative, so He chose Moses and sent Him to tell them of His offer of a wonderful Chuppah, a land of milk and honey (a veritable Garden of Eden). Would they want to come and be intimate with Him in this land? And so began God's next phase in His quest for a Bride.

Once this people accepted the offer that Moses, God's representative made, God began the process of negotiation with Pharaoh for the Mohar, the Bride price. What would it take for Pharaoh to let His people go? When Moses said to Pharaoh that God had said to "let my people go", at that point Pharaoh could have said, "What will your God give me?" Instead, Pharaoh flatly refused to even negotiate. He would not let God's people go for any amount.

Next, we see how God is willing to go to every extent to rescue the one He loves. Although Pharaoh will not be reasonable, God will not be denied the one who has accepted His proposal. Through a series of plagues, God breaks the will of Pharaoh through the decimation of the land of Egypt. God is literally about to take His bride out of the hands of Pharaoh and translate them out of Pharaoh's kingdom into His kingdom.

There is yet one thing that must be established in the mind and the heart of God. Are these people serious about their acceptance of His tenaim (His conditions)?

Pharaoh would not set a value on this people (a mohar). Indeed, Pharaoh didn't value them at all, they were only good for him as slaves. Therefore, since Pharaoh would not accept God's request for a Bride price, God Himself sets the Bride's price (the Mohar) and asks the Israelites to demonstrate their willingness to go with Him by symbolically accepting this Mohar themselves by placing the blood of a lamb over the doorposts of their homes. Those that did not put the blood over the door would be in effect saying that they would rather suffer the fate of the Egyptians than to be married to God.

This would be later called Passover because God said that when He saw the blood, He would pass over them. This word Passover in Hebrew is Pesach (פֶּסַח pronounced Pay' sakh). Literally, then, God was saying that when He saw the blood, He would "Pesach" (pass over) them. This Hebrew word is used in another Bible passage and may help us to understand what happened in this moment of Israel's history.

Isaiah 31:5 *"Like birds flying about, so will the LORD of hosts defend Jerusalem. Defending, He will also deliver it; **Passing over**, He will preserve it."* The two words," Passing over", is the word Pesach in Hebrew.

We often think of Passover as the time when God skipped the houses of those who had the blood on them and visited the houses where the blood was not on them. However, by comparing this Scripture with the account in Exodus, we see that Passover is a picture of a someone who, like a bird, is flying over those very homes and protecting them with its wings. So, then, the death angel was passing through Egypt visiting the homes and someone other than the death angel was hovering over to protect those homes which had the blood applied.

189

This is a beautiful picture of the protection that is symbolized by the wearing of the tallit. Psalm 91 says, *"He that dwells in the secret place of the Most High shall abide under the shadow of the Almighty"*. The "secret place" is the Holy of Holies that is represented in the tallit. Can you see how coming into your own personal Holy of Holies by putting on the tallit causes the shadow of the wings of the Almighty to hover over you in protection?

After leaving Egypt, Israel travels to Mount Sinai. Here they are given the Ketubah which becomes what we know as the Torah or the Five Books of Moses. Now Israel is formally betrothed. We may know this as Shavuot or, as it is called in Greek, Pentecost.

Pesach (with its accompanying feasts of Unleavened Bread and First Fruits) and Shavuot make up the Spring Feasts. There are three more feasts that are established by God for the Jewish people. These last three feasts are rehearsals for the final wedding (the Nisuin). Between Pentecost and the fall feasts the bride (the Church) is to get herself ready. At the same time the groom (Yeshua) is preparing the honeymoon suite (the Chuppah) where they will spend seven years together.

The next Feast on God's calendar is the Feast of Trumpets (Yom Teruah). This represents the catching away of the bride. Every year, God rehearses this event. One day soon it no longer will be a rehearsal. The day of His appearing is very soon. We are watching and waiting for Him to come and take us with Him. This will be our wedding day!

Along with the Feast of Trumpets is the Day of Atonement (Yom Kippur). Just as in the Jewish wedding the bride and groom are considered to have their personal Yom Kippur and all their past sins are taken away, so we will begin our new life with Him. He will take us into His Chuppah and we will enjoy the marriage supper of the Lamb for seven years.

When Yeshua drank of the wine with His disciples, He took the last cup and told His disciples that He would not drink of that cup until He drank it anew with us in His Father's Kingdom. Even on the cross He refused the wine that they offered Him (Mark 15:23). He is waiting for us in order to share that cup with us.

The last Feast is the Feast of Tabernacles. This represents where we will come back to earth to live for 1000 years. Yeshua will be our King and we will be His Queen.

Through the years, Israel was unfaithful and eventually God gave them a writ of divorce and then forced them out of their land into captivity. This is very similar to when Adam and Eve were cast out of the Garden of Eden. This is known in the Bible as the Babylonian and the Assyrian captivity.

Nevertheless, God gave them a promise that He would bring them back into the land. This is another way of saying that He would enter back into a state of betrothal if they would accept Him again. He even said that He would heal their backslidings (Hosea 14:4; Jeremiah 3:22). In addition, He promised that there would be a day when He would write the Law (the Torah) upon their hearts (Jeremiah 31; Isaiah 59:21)

1,000 years after the giving of the Law (Torah) on Mount Sinai, an event happened that was so momentous that it changed the way we record history. "In the fullness of time, God sent forth His Son."

Up until this time God had always made His proposal of marriage through a representative. Everything up to this point was only a shadow, a type. Every prophecy, every Feast day, every promise, every expectation was now here in the flesh.

Yeshua came to take a bride. For 3 ½ years He demonstrated his love for the one He wanted to win. He healed the sick, He cleansed the leper, He cast out devils, He spoke blessings over children, He raised the dead, and He preached Good News to the poor.

191

At Gethsemane, he negotiated the Mohar (the bride's price). Yeshua prayed, "*O My Father, if it is possible, let this cup pass from Me; nevertheless, not as I will, but as You will.*" However, the price could not be decreased. The Bride was worth too much! The Bride had incredible value! This was no ordinary Bride; this was the best of all God's creation! However, the Bride must submit her total being to the one who would pay this price. She must apply the blood to her heart so that Yeshua would "Pesach" her (i.e. cast His wing over her in protection).

At Calvary, the Mohar was paid. At Calvary, we become betrothed to Yeshua. After His Resurrection He showed Himself alive for 40 days. He then disappeared out of sight. However, He left us a promise that He would come again in like manner to consummate the marriage through Nisuin.

He gave us gifts (Matan). Ten days after He left, in an upper room, the Holy Spirit descended in much the same way as God descended on Mount Sinai when the Torah was given. On that day of Pentecost, the Torah was placed on our hearts. The Ketubah was written not on tables of stone but on the heart of flesh.

We are waiting for that day when the shofar will sound and a shout will be made, "The Bridegroom comes!" We are looking forward to the Nisuin where we will spend seven years in the Chuppah enjoying the Marriage Supper of the Lamb.

In the meantime, we spend time in His presence in our personal Chuppah, our prayer shawl. Though this is only a material representation of a grander spiritual reality, it is a little bit of Heaven that we can enjoy today. In this life we "see through a glass darkly", but then we shall see face to face.

Chapter Twelve
Blessings Under The Tallit

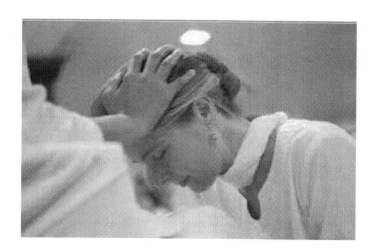

Genesis 27:34-38 *"When Esau heard the words of his father, he cried with an exceedingly great and bitter cry, and said to his father, "Bless me – me also, O my father!"*

But he said, "Your brother came with deceit and has taken away your blessing."

And Esau said, "Is he not rightly named Jacob? For he has supplanted me these two times. He took away my birthright, and now look, he has taken away my blessing!" And he said, "Have you not reserved a blessing for me?"

Then Isaac answered and said to Esau, "Indeed I have made him your master, and all his brethren I have given to him as servants; with grain and wine I have sustained him. What shall I do now for you, my son?"

And Esau said to his father, "Have you only one blessing, my father? Bless me – me also, O my father!" And Esau lifted up his voice and wept."

The Hebrew word for "birthright" is בכורה (pronounced bek-oh-raw', transliterated as bekorah). The Hebrew word for blessing is ברכה (pronounced bare'-ah-kah, transliterated as berakah). These two words are very similar because they share the same Hebrew root word ברך (pronounced bah-rahk', transliterated as barak). Barak means to kneel, bless, praise, salute. It also has a connotation of giving a gift with humility.

The birthright and the blessing represented the covenant that God had given to Abraham that was to be passed down from oldest son to oldest son. This became known as the birthright blessing, or bekorah berakah.

The birthright blessing is of paramount importance in Biblical history. When a father would become elderly or frail, or when he felt it was time to confer the blessing, he would call his children to him and, under a special mantle (in later Biblical times, a prayer shawl), he would place his hands on them and bless them.

This birthright blessing was a transference of the blessings of Abraham both spiritual and material. It meant that the one being blessed would be the one from whom the Messiah would come. It would also mean that the promised land of Abraham (the land of Israel) would belong to them. Therefore, the event of the birthright blessing was the fulfillment of a lifetime of anticipation.

When that moment came, it was a solemn, most holy, experience. The father, who would bestow the blessing, would be in prayer waiting for the Spirit of God to come upon him in order to properly transfer the spiritual blessing upon his son. It was the most important time that a father and son could ever have together.

The blessing was also prophetic. Because the father would be under the influence of God's Spirit, the words he spoke over his son would define the son's future. Therefore, to not get this blessing would be the worst possible time in a son's life.

The birthright also meant that the son who received the blessing would receive a double portion of all the father had. How this worked was that the father would count how many sons he had and then add one to the number. So a father who had two sons (as in Esau and Jacob) would divide his assets into three parts and give to the one with the birthright two-thirds and the other son would get one-third.

All this makes us realize how great a disappointment Esau would have endured. It was at this moment that Esau realized, too late, just how valuable his birthright was. However, he had already given up his right to the birthright to his twin brother Jacob for a bowl of red lentil soup. Now he accuses his brother of "taking away" his birthright and also "taking" his blessing. In reality, it was Esau who was trying to "take away" what he had given to his brother Jacob.

However, you cannot read this Scripture without feeling sorry for Esau. He had sold his birthright to Jacob. Now his father Isaac had blessed Jacob thinking that he was blessing Esau.

Most people, when reading this account in Scripture will assume that the blessing and the birthright were one and the same. Indeed, up to this point in Jewish history they were combined.

What Isaac tried to do was to separate the blessing and birthright and circumvent God's will. Isaac loved Esau. However, Isaac knew that Esau had sold his birthright. He also knew that God had prophesied over the two boys while still in Rebekah's womb that the older would serve the younger. Still, Isaac wanted to give something to Esau. Therefore, we see Isaac attempting a plan to separate the blessing from the birthright.

However, Rebekah loved Jacob. When Rebekah heard Isaac telling Esau that he wanted to give him the blessing, she immediately put a plan into place to prevent this. In the course of events, Jacob ends up receiving not only the blessing but also the birthright.

Most Bible commentators say that Jacob "stole" the blessing. However, you cannot "steal" that which is yours. In fact, it was Esau, in conjunction with his father Isaac, who was attempting to cheat Jacob out of what was rightfully his. Esau had despised his birthright. Esau gave it away. Now Isaac and Esau are trying to defraud Jacob from what is rightfully his. Rebekah takes the steps she feels is necessary to upset Isaac's plan.

Genesis 27:15 says, *"And Rebekah took goodly raiment of her eldest son Esau, which were with her in the house, and put them upon Jacob her younger son."* This was a special garment that Isaac must have given to Esau not only because he was the elder son but also because Isaac loved Esau.

This reminds me of a later time when Jacob would also give a special garment to Joseph, whom he loved, to show that Joseph was going to be given the birthright. We know this as Joseph's coat of many colors. However, the translation of the Hebrew does not mention the word "colors". Instead, it is better translated "a coat of distinction". I have written about this in detail in another chapter of this book.

Because the blessing is such an important occasion, the son would wear a special garment for the occasion. When Jacob came in to his father (who was blind) not only did he have his hands and back of his neck covered with goat skins to fool his father into believing he was Esau, he also wore Esau's special mantle. When Isaac brought Jacob close to him, he smelled the smell of the field on the mantle and deduced that this must indeed be Esau, all the while it was really Jacob in disguise. Consequently, Jacob received the blessing that was rightfully his, but one which his father had intended for Esau.

We may not like what Rebekah and Jacob did. However, there is no mention either in the Old Testament or in the New Testament of God's disapproval of Jacob or Rebekah. We do have several mentions of God's disapproval of Esau and his despising of the birthright.

After realizing that he had blessed Jacob instead of Esau, Isaac shook violently. He was visibly shaken after realizing that he had been opposing God Himself. Isaac knew that the Spirit of the Lord had been present during the blessing and that it was the Lord's will and intent all along to bless Jacob instead of Esau. Had God not wanted Jacob blessed, God would have stopped the blessing Himself. Isaac knew that if God wanted to intervene, He certainly could have. After all, He intervened with his father Abraham when he was much younger laying on the altar of sacrifice.

Esau begs his father three times to give him a blessing as well. Isaac eventually does pronounce a blessing on Esau. However, the Hebrew actually records the blessing as really a curse over Esau. Genesis 27:38-40 (LEB) *"Your home shall be from the fatness of the land, and from the dew of heaven above. But by your sword you shall live, and you shall serve your brother. But it shall be that when free yourself you shall tear off his yoke from your neck."* This makes Esau extremely angry and he vows to kill his twin brother Jacob as soon as his father dies.

It is interesting that Esau earlier did not care for his birthright. Now he is willing to commit murder in order to get it back. This is how much the birthright blessing really meant to Esau. It is unfortunate for Esau that he did not realize how much he wanted the birthright when he was asked to sell it.

Even though the Scripture describes the emotions of Isaac and Esau so vividly, I do not feel sorry for Esau. I also do not feel sorry for Isaac. Their plan to circumvent God's plan for all of their lives left them in a precarious position.

I wonder, if Isaac and Esau had not opposed God's will, if Esau would have gotten a blessing instead of the curse that he received. I am reminded of Abraham after God told him that Isaac would be the son of promise. Abraham asked God for a blessing for his other son Ishmael. God blessed Ishmael as well as Isaac. Even though Isaac received all of Abraham's wealth, Ishmael did not seem to be resentful to Isaac. Both Isaac and Ishmael were at the funeral of their father Abraham. Both sons buried their father. Although there was animosity before this time, we hear of no animosity between the two boys after the blessing is given. It is unfortunate that the same cannot be said about Esau and Jacob.

There is something remarkable that occurs within the text of the story of these two boys, Esau and Jacob. You can only see this in the Hebrew. Prior to the selling of the birthright, both Esau and Jacob have the Hebrew letters את (Aleph-Tav) before each of their names. The last time we see the Aleph-Tav before Esau's name is on the day that Isaac asked Esau to hunt some savory meat so that he might bless Esau as the first born. After this, the Aleph-Tav never appears again in front of Esau's name but only in front of Jacob's name.

The letters Aleph-Tav mean "The strength of the covenant" in ancient Hebrew pictograph. This indicates that "the strength of the covenant" was on both boys until that fateful day and then only Jacob has the Aleph-Tav before his name. This seems to indicate that God had it in His plan to bless both boys as He did Isaac and Ishmael earlier, but Esau forfeited his blessing by his contempt.

With Esau angry at his brother Jacob and his plans to kill him, Rebekah goes to Isaac to ask him to sent Jacob away. She couches the request with the observation that Jacob should find a wife among her own people. Isaac then summons Jacob and then gives him the birthright and sends him on his way.

Genesis 28:3-4 *"May God Almighty (El Shaddai) bless you, and make you fruitful and multiply you, that you may be an assembly of peoples; and give you the blessing of Abraham, to you and your descendants with you, that you may inherit the land in which you are a stranger, which God gave to Abraham."*

Years pass, Jacob marries Leah and Rachel. His wife Rachel has two sons Joseph and Benjamin. Leah, Bilhah, and Zilpah have the other 10 sons and one daughter of Jacob. Joseph is sold by his brothers into Egypt. More years pass eventually Joseph's brothers and his father move to Egypt and join Joseph.

As time goes on, Jacob comes to the end of his life. Like his father Isaac before him, he calls his sons before him in order to bless them. First of all, comes Joseph. However, Joseph does not seek the blessing for himself. Instead Joseph brings his two boys Manasseh and Ephraim to his father Jacob.

When the boys are in front of Jacob, he crosses his hands and blesses the younger over the older. What is remarkable is that Manasseh does not seem to mind that his younger brother Ephraim is honored above him.

Perhaps Joseph, remembering his growing up with resentful brothers had determined that his boys would not ever have those feelings toward each other and had raised them accordingly. At any rate, this quality is recognized even today as a Jewish father blesses his son and says "May you be as Ephraim and Manasseh". In fact, the Scripture says that fathers would say those very words.

Genesis 48:20 *"So he blessed them that day, saying, "By you Israel will bless, saying, "May God make you as Ephraim and as Manasseh!" And thus he set Ephraim before Manasseh."*

Paul, in writing to the church at Philippi, echoed this same sentiment.

Philippian 2:3 *"Let nothing be done through selfish ambition or conceit, but in lowliness of mind let each esteem others better than himself."*

Therefore, Ephraim received the spiritual blessing, but not the birthright. The birthright would have belonged to Jacob's firstborn son, Reuben. However, Reuben had forfeited his birthright. The birthright would have then passed to Simeon but he and the next younger son Levi also forfeited their birthright. This brings us to Judah.

When Jacob puts his hand on each of his sons, the Spirit of the Lord speaks a prophecy over each son. When Judah comes forth, Jacob prophesies a kingdom would arise out of his children. Specifically, these words were said:

Genesis 49:10 *"The scepter shall not depart from Judah, nor a lawgiver from between his feet, until Shiloh comes; and to Him shall be the obedience of the people."*

So now Judah receives the birthright in the form of a promise of ruling as a king over his other brothers until Messiah (who is referred here as Shiloh) comes.

Yeshua is of the tribe of Judah. He is called the Lion of the tribe of Judah. Yeshua is Shiloh!

Another extensive topic is to follow Ephraim who eventually becomes part of the Northern Kingdom and Judah who becomes part of the Southern Kingdom. The nation of Israel is divided after the death of Solomon when Rehoboam and Jeroboam split the kingdom.

The Southern Kingdom (Judah) goes into Babylonian captivity and eventually returns back to the land of Israel. The Northern Kingdom also goes into captivity to the Assyrians but never return. Instead they assimilate with the nations that they are dispersed into. They lose their identity and are referred to as the "lost tribes of Israel".

Because of their complete assimilation with Gentile people, Ephraim is inextricably connected with Gentiles. It is even safe to assume that Ephraim now represents the Gentiles.

The prophets prophesied that one day the stick of Ephraim would reunite with the stick of Judah and they would become one stick (Ezekiel 37:19). This is exactly what Paul was referring to when he talked about the "one new man" (Ephesians 2:14-18), Gentile (Ephraim) and Jew (Judah) becoming one in Christ (Messiah).

So much can be written about this, however it is outside the scope of this book. It is enough that I have shown how the blessing is now with Ephraim (Gentile believers) and the birthright is with Judah (Jewish believers). If we are to see the fulness of the birthright blessing, we must unite with the Jewish believers in Yeshua.

Jewish fathers today call their children to them every Sabbath and bless them. Every week the boys hear "May you be like Ephraim and Manasseh" and the girls hear "May you be like Rachel and Leah". These are the role models for Jewish children to learn to honor each other and to not allow jealousy to disrupt the family.

There is one more type of blessing to be covered in this chapter. This blessing is referred to as the "priestly blessing". Moses was told by God to have Aaron and his sons say specific words over the people of Israel. They were not to say what they wanted to say, they had to speak the exact words that Yahweh told them to speak.

Century after century, these words are repeated over and over. This is continued even today. This blessing is awesome in its power to transform individuals, families and nations!

Numbers 6:22-27 *"And the LORD spoke to Moses, saying: "Speak to Aaron and his sons, saying, this is the way you shall bless the children of Israel. Say to them:*

The LORD bless you and keep you; the LORD make His face shine upon you, and be gracious to you; the LORD lift up His countenance upon you, and give you peace."

So they shall put My Name on the children of Israel, and I will bless them."

In Hebraic culture, a person's name is more than just an identifier. The name is a description of the qualities that the person should emanate. Therefore, a name would give insight into a person's character and personality. To know someone's name would to be to know who they are intimately and relationally.

Therefore, when God said to Moses, *"So they shall put My Name on the children of Israel"*, He was saying that they would be putting His personality and His character on them. The Priestly blessing then would be a life changing blessing when it was repeated over and over on a person's life.

You can see then why it became one of the most important events in an Israeli's life when the Priest would recite these words over a congregation. They would cover themselves with their prayer shawls, entering into their personal Holy of Holies and receive those words as if God Himself was saying them. They would concentrate on every word as the Priest would sing (in a kind of chanting sound) every syllable of each Hebrew word. They would rock forwards and backwards in order to create a trance-like state in order to focus more intently on the words themselves. They would be aware that Yahweh's personality and character was being formed within them as they heard the words. It was powerful. It was life-changing.

In addition to the Priests saying the blessing over the nation of Israel, each father would also speak these blessings over each of their children on the Sabbath after the Sabbath dinner on Friday night.

The Sabbath dinner itself was a special event in the week. Everything for the Sabbath would be prepared the day before. This is called the "preparation day". They would take out the very best china, every week. They would bake a very special bread called Challah, which they would break and pass to each person. They would wear their best clothes. They would put out the best table settings. The Sabbath was an honored "guest" in their home.

This all was to teach them about a Messiah (one who was the Sabbath itself) who would come someday and knock on their door in order to "sup with them". It was, and is, a dress rehearsal for receiving Messiah into their hearts and enjoying with Him the best of their lives. It is interesting that the Hebrew word for house or home is the same word for a person's body. Therefore, welcoming the "Sabbath" into a home is easily seen to represent welcoming Yeshua, our Sabbath, into our hearts, the center of our body. Revelation 3:20 says this beautifully for every Jewish person to comprehend.

"Behold, I stand at the door and knock. If anyone hears My voice and opens the door, I will come in to him and dine with him, and he with Me."

When you begin to understand the Hebraic roots behind the Scripture, it brings a depth of meaning that was not there before. We so need our Jewish brothers to come to know Yeshua HaMaschiach and their Savior. We need them to help complete us as Yeshua completes them. We speak of Jewish converts as "completed Jews", actually, it is us Gentiles who are being "completed" when we embrace the richness of the Jewish community.

After the dinner, the father would call each of his children to him and, one by one, would place his hands on their head and bless them. If the child is a boy, he would begin with "May you be like Ephraim and Manasseh". If the child is a girl, he would begin with "May you be like Rebekah, Leah, and Rachel". Then he would speak the Priestly blessing over them.

"Yahweh will bless you and keep you.

Yahweh will make his face shine upon you and be gracious to you.

Yahweh will lift His countenance upon you and give you peace."

(Because the name Yahweh is considered too holy to utter out loud, the Jewish father would substitute the name Adonai, which means Lord. I have put "Yahweh" here because that is exactly what the Priestly blessing says is His name in Hebrew.)

After speaking this blessing, it is also customary to add your own special words of encouragement, praise, or even your desire for them. Then the father would hug and kiss each child and then bless the next in line.

This affirmation of love from the father every Friday evening cannot help but have an impact upon the children's lives. If a father does this blessing while wearing the prayer shawl, it adds the wonderful teaching of being under the protective wing of the father as well as the protective wing of God.

The importance of the blessing is that it gives us our identity. In this day where children do not even know if they are a girl or a boy, correct identity is vital. Identity determines your destiny. The blessing is a declaration which empowers someone to succeed. Under the curse, you diminish; things flow away from you. Under the blessing, you increase, things flow into you.

We can establish a culture of blessing within our home. If generational curses can be passed on to our children, then why not create some generational blessings that can be passed as well. Why not speak over your children's children and grandchildren even before they are born. In the Bible, Balaam could not curse Israel, though Balak paid him a lot of money to do so (Numbers 23).

Of all the tools God gave you to raise a child, the most powerful is your tongue. Why not start a family blessing tradition in your home? You can enhance the experience by wearing a prayer shawl as you bless your child. You will speak the future into existence with your child.

When you speak the Priestly blessing over your child you are actually allowing God to bless your child through you. The last part of the verse I quoted in this section says, *"So they shall put My Name on the children of Israel, and I will bless them."* This indicates that God Himself is blessing them when you speak these words over them.

I believe that once you begin to implement this tradition of blessing your children that God will also give you words to speak that will shape their future. The Scripture says, *"For I know the thoughts that I think toward you, says the LORD, thoughts of peace and not of evil, to give you a future and a hope."*

God never runs out of great things to say about you or your children. He has an infinite amount of positive thoughts that He would love to express but he needs your tongue to speak them out over your child. Just think about this Scripture for a moment.

Psalm 139:17-18 *"How precious also are Your thoughts to me, O God! How great is the sum of them! If I should count them, they would be more in number than the sand."*

God's thoughts about us are more than all the grains of sand! How much is that? Well, a group of researchers at the University of Hawaii tried to calculate the number of grains of sand. Without getting into all the technical elements of their study they said,

"If you assume a grain of sand has an average size and you calculate how many grains are in a teaspoon and then multiply by all the beaches and deserts in the world, the Earth has roughly (and we're speaking very roughly here) 7.5X10¹⁸ grains of sand, or seven quintillion, five hundred quadrillion grains."

That number would look like this: 7,500,000,000,000,000,000. That is a lot of grains! That is a lot of thoughts that God has for us! We really need to get busy allowing God to speak His thoughts through us into our children!

Now, you may think that, even for God, that is a lot of separate thoughts. Does God really have that many different thoughts about us? I mean, isn't He just speaking metaphorically? Well, let's look at another Scripture.

Luke 12:7 *"But the very hairs of your head are all numbered. Do not fear therefore; you are of more value than many sparrows."*

Hair is mentioned over 100 times in the Bible, often in the context of God's loving care and protection for His people. For example, When God delivered Shadrach, Meshach, and Abednego from the fiery furnace, "the hair of their head was not singed" (Daniel 3:27). In Luke 21:18, Jesus warned His disciples of persecution but told them not to fear because "not a hair of your head shall be lost". In Luke 12:7 He says that "the very hairs of your head are numbered." How personally and intimately our Savior knows and loves us!

The human head has an estimated 100,000 hairs, though the number varies from person to person. So, compared to sand, it seems relatively easier for God to know the number of hairs than He would know the number of His thoughts about us.

But now consider this Scripture. Psalm 147:4 *"He counts the number of the stars; He calls them all by name."*

How many stars are there? Well, it appears that scientists have estimated, with the assistance of the Hubble telescope, this vast number. When we consider distant galaxies, faint stars, red dwarfs, and everything we have ever recorded in the sky, and we have an astronomical number! There are 70 sextillion stars in the observable universe. That number would look like this: 70,000,000,000,000,000,000,000. God calls them all by name! That is roughly 10 times more than the grains of sand. However, we have not discovered all of the galaxies as of yet!

So, if God counts the stars and knows them all by name and counts the hair on our head, He could undoubtedly have the number of thoughts about us that He says He has. We are His prize creation; He loves us so very much!

So that brings us back to the Priestly blessing given under a prayer shawl. What exactly does this Priestly blessing do? We have already looked at the fact that we get a deposit of Yahweh's character and personality with the blessing, but what is the blessing?

The Priestly blessing is often referred to as the three-in-one blessing. It is expressed in the singular not the plural. This highlights the application of the blessing to each individual not simply a group. The following is the Priestly blessing written in Hebrew:

יברכך יהוה וישמרך

יאר יהוה פניו אליך ויחנך

ישא יהוה פניו אליך וישם לך שלום

The three parts of the blessing written in Hebrew have 3 words in the first section, 5 words in the second section, and 7 words in the third section. These total 15 words. Each section has two parts connected with the word "and", which in Hebrew is only one letter (ו, vav) added to the beginning of a word.

Let's look at the previous numbers as they represent the number of words. In the beginning of this book I set out a list of numbers with their meanings. The number 3 is the number of the Godhead, Divine completeness, and perfect testimony. The number 5 is the number of grace, the cross, atonement, and life. The number 7 is the number of spiritual completion and perfection.

Therefore, using Biblical numerology we have a description of the message contained within the Priestly blessing through numbers. The message would be as follows:

"The Godhead with perfect testimony by grace through the cross brings spiritual completion and perfection."

When we look at the number 15, which is the total number of the Hebrew words, we see another aspect of the Priestly blessing. The number 15 is a product of 10 + 5. The number 10 is written as the Hebrew letter ׳ (yod, pronounced yood). The number 5 is written as the Hebrew letter ה (heh, pronounced hay). These two letters put together form the word יה (Yah). The word Yah is an abbreviated form of the name יהוה (Yahweh). Therefore, when God told Moses that by saying this blessing the Priests would be putting His Name on them, He was actually doing just that!

Now let us look at the English translation and look into the deeper meaning of each of the three sections. Each section is in two parts so we will look at that as well.

"The LORD bless you and keep you."

The word "bless" in the first part of this section is the Hebrew word בָּרַך (barak, pronounced bah-rahk'). This word for bless means to kneel with the intent of offering a gift. It is a blessing for material success and flourishing.

The second part "and keep you" is a promise that the blessing will be protected. Not only will Yahweh bless you with material success He will also protect that material success from loss.

"The LORD make His face to shine on you and be gracious to you".

While the first section was a promise of material success, this section is a promise of spiritual success. It is a promise of spiritual enlightenment that you may understand the correct path to choose.

The second part "and be gracious to you" uses the Hebrew word חֵן (chen, pronounced khen). This word is translated "grace", but also means "favor". Not only will Yahweh give you spiritual enlightenment so that you may understand the path to choose, He will also give you His Divine Favor after you choose that path.

209

"The LORD lift His countenance toward you and give you peace."

This section speaks of the Lord "lifting his face". This signifies that the Lord is lifting his face in order to look you eye to eye, face to face. This is a picture of respect as a friend would respect His friend. This is a promise that Yahweh will be a friend to you and treat you always with respect.

The last part of this section speaks about peace, shalom. The word "give", as in "give you peace", means to set, to establish you in peace. The Lord just doesn't give you peace and leave it at that. He sees to it that you are firmly established in peace (shalom).

The word that is translated "peace" is the Hebrew word "shalom" (שלום, pronounced shah-lohm'). Shalom means health, welfare, security, justice, and tranquility, also freedom from all disaster.

When you look at the individual letters of the Hebrew word shalom, you find an interesting bit of information. If you remember, I said in an earlier chapter that when you take the individual meanings of the letters in a Hebrew word you end up with a "story" of what that word does.

Shalom is written in Hebrew as, שלום. Let's look at the letters. ש in Paleo-Hebrew is W and is a picture of teeth and means "to destroy". ל in Paleo-Hebrew is (and is a picture of a shepherd's staff and means "authority". ו in Paleo-Hebrew is Y and is a picture of a tent peg, or nail and means "to establish". ם in Paleo-Hebrew is ל and means "chaos". Therefore, when you put these individual meanings of the letters together you get the "story" of the word shalom. You will experience shalom when you "destroy the authority that establishes chaos". You may still have the chaos around you, but when the "authority" has been destroyed you have a peaceful attitude inside. Nothing or no one can take your health, welfare, security, justice, or tranquility unless you give them the "authority" to do so.

Yeshua would have undoubtedly used this priestly blessing when he called the little children to him. It is a common practice for Rabbi's to bless children with this particular blessing. Yeshua would have drawn each child individually to Him and wrapped his arm, with the prayer shawl, around them and spoke the blessing over each of them. I certainly can imagine that Yeshua would have also given a personal prophetic message over each child as well.

You can visualize how much time this might have taken. No wonder the disciples wanted to keep the children away from Yeshua. However, Yeshua would not have it. He said, "Allow the little children to come to me and forbid them not".

This demonstrates vividly how much Yeshua wants to bless each and every one of us. He wants us to hear the words of the priestly blessing and He wants to speak prophetic words into our ears. He needs a voice in this world in order to do that. He is residing on the inside of us. We are His voice. When we take the prayer shawl and bring individuals under its wings and speak this blessing, He will speak through us a prophetic message to that person. You could do this without the prayer shawl but how much more meaningful this is when we implement the teaching tool that He has given us.

When Yeshua left earth to return to Heaven, He blessed His disciples. There are clues in the Scripture that makes it plain that He must have spoken the priestly blessing as He was leaving. Here is the Scripture in question.

Luke 24:50-51 *"And He led them out as far as Bethany, and He lifted up His hands and blessed them. Now it came to pass, while He blessed them, that He was parted from them and carried up into heaven."*

"He lifted up His hands and blessed them". When the Priests speak the priestly blessing they put their hands over their heads and each hand forms the letter "shin" (שׁ).

The letter "shin" not only means "to destroy", as we saw in the word "shalom", but also may mean "passion, desire, fire, or protection". The hands are then put together to make 5 openings which speak of "grace". The openings are understood to represent the windows of Heaven that God would look through in order to bless them. So we have "protective grace coming from the Father in Heaven" being symbolized as the priestly blessing is said.

As Yeshua was ascending into Heaven, He is pronouncing the priestly blessing upon His disciples. No wonder that it says in the next verse that "they returned to Jerusalem with great joy."

The Priestly Blessing is also a Parenting Guide. If you have been looking for a simple and concise guidebook on parenting, then look no further! Here in three simple statements is a wonderful exhortation to parents on how to be effective parents to their children.

By imitating God and His specific ways of dealing with us, as described in the Priestly Blessing, we will be successful as parents. These statements present an expression of love for the child, an impartation of faith for their future, and (as we have learned) literally puts His identity and His personality upon our children. Let us then look at the implications contained within these three statements.

The first statement speaks of blessing and keeping. *"The LORD bless you and keep you"*. This speaks about nurturing and safeguarding.

This attitude toward your child begins in the womb. The mother must watch her diet and her habits, for the sake of the baby. The father takes special care of the mother, because of the baby.

After the baby is born, we put up barriers for safety. Special cribs are purchased. Pets are watched and kept from harming the infant. As they grow, we fix cabinet doors so they cannot be opened by the child. We never leave them alone near a pool or in a grocery cart. We are ever present to make sure they are protected.

Also, we give them what they need to grow. We pour love on them in copious amounts! We kiss them incessantly! We talk to them. We tell them that we love them. We also provide education for them, we buy toys that will educate and train. We provide food, clothing, and anything they need for comfort.

We are constantly nurturing and safeguarding them throughout their growing up years. They need us and we give ourselves wholeheartedly to their welfare. This is some of the greatest moments in our lives with them. You have the greatest of hopes for your wonderful child. You are wondering just what your child will become. You have positive aspirations for them to succeed. You are very proud parents indeed!

The second part of the Priestly Blessing gives us the next step in the parenting process. *"The LORD will make His face shine upon you and be gracious to you"*. This speaks of acceptance, approval, and unconditional love.

This process begins at the birth of the child. Before birth, the child cannot see your face. However, once the child is born, you look into that beautiful face of your child and you do what every parent has ever done, you smile! You can't help it! Babies make you smile! They are such a wonderful creation of God! Everyone who looks at the baby does the same thing! They smile!

Your face lights up with a brightness that is unmistakable! Your child for the first time sees you and what he, or she, sees is your smile! That smile then is indelibly placed in that child's mind and it will be that smile that will be a motivating factor all through their life. They want and need your smile.

Not only do they need your smile on their life, they also need your unconditional love. The last part of that statement mentions the word "gracious". Grace is defined as "unmerited favor".

You are just happy with your child. You like the child just the way they are. They don't have to do anything; they are just totally perfect. When they do their first drawing, you rave about how beautiful and wonderful it is. You put it on the refrigerator. When company comes, you retrieve it and pass it around to everyone. You brag on your child. No one has ever had a child as wonderful as yours!

In the first part, the nurturing and safeguarding, you are looking forward to the future. In the second part, the acceptance, approval, and unconditional love, you are looking only at the present.

At each stage of their life, you continue to do the same thing. You smile! When they are in the Terrific Twos, you smile! When they are in the Tremendous Threes, you smile! When they are in the Fabulous Fours, you smile! On and on, even through the Adventurous Teens into adulthood, you smile! It is what makes your child thrive! It is what your child needs more than anything else from you.

Then we come to the final stage that is expressed in *"The LORD will lift His countenance upon you and give you peace."* This speaks of respect and release.

Up until now, you have been above the child, looking down on them. You have been in control. Now, they have grown and you are looking them eye to eye.

The adult stage is when you have the greatest possibility of disappointment. The child may make choices that you do not like or choose a path that you would not choose for them. Your eyes are downcast. You may want to try to control them through your disapproval. This is called "putting the guilt trip" on them.

This Scripture suggests a very different approach. You lift your countenance, your face. This suggests that the child has grown up. No longer are you above the child looking down at him. You are now looking at an adult; one who can make his or her own choices, just like you. You lift up your face and you give them peace. You let your child go. You accept their choices and stop trying to control them through guilt. You treat them as more of an equal.

This is, without question, the hardest part of parenting. Cutting the apron strings, is never easy. We have cared for them for so long. We want the best for them now. When they make choices that seem unsafe, we want to shelter them. When they choose paths that seem fraught with failure, we want to rescue them. But now, they are grown. It is really hard to accept. But accept, we must, if our child is to continue to be healthy in their relationship with us.

The child's greatest need from you now is peace. It is a gift that you give to them. It is a gift that they will cherish as long as they live.

So, we have moved from nurturing and safeguarding, to acceptance, approval, and unconditional love, and now to respect and release. It has been a long journey. If we are fortunate, our reward will come when our child has children.

Grandchildren are the reward for raising a child. If this wonderful event has not happened for you, let me assure you, there is nothing on this earth as wonderful and as rewarding as a grandchild. They are absolutely the best!

Chapter Thirteen

The Skirt (Hem) Of Him That Is A Jew

Zechariah 8:23 (KJV) *"Thus saith the LORD of hosts; In those days it shall come to pass, that ten men shall take hold out of all languages of the nations, even shall take hold of the skirt of him that is a Jew, saying, "We will go with you: for we have heard that God is with you."*

The phrase "the skirt of him that is a Jew" is a phenomenal prophecy. We will look at this as we continue in this chapter.

The word "skirt" in Hebrew is כָּנָף (transliterated as kanaph and pronounced kah-nahf'). The word "kanaph" is translated skirt, corner, wing, hem, or lock (as in hair). The tassels (or tzitzit) are tied on the four corners (the four kanaphs) of a garment. So, when this verse says that "ten men...out of all languages of the nations...shall take hold of the skirt of Him that is a Jew", it is saying that they will take hold of the corner of that Jew's garment. In doing so, they take hold of the tzitzit that is tied to the corner.

Who are these ten men? During the Babylonian Captivity a new type of worship began. The Temple in Jerusalem was destroyed and the Kingdom of Judah was in captivity in Babylon. Because they no longer could offer physical sacrifices in Jerusalem, the leaders began to worship in small groups called synagogues. In order for the synagogue to be established, they would have to have ten eligible men who were at least Bar Mitzvah age or older. This quorum of men were representative of the whole congregation. Therefore, Zechariah in writing this verse would have assumed that those that read his prophecy in that day would understand that the "ten men" would be a representative number for the masses of men, women, and children of every nation and every language of the earth. It is we, who have been divorced from our Hebrew roots, that have difficulty understanding this passage.

Notice, however, that they take hold of the corner of the garment of only one Jew. A particular Jew. A Jew who has "God with Him". They say that they will go "with Him", because they "heard that God is with Him".

Since these men are from every nation and language, it is obvious that this is speaking of Gentiles. Therefore, it is the Gentiles

220

(men and women, represented by the 10 men) who are grasping the corner of a man who is a Jew and saying that they will go with Him.

When Jewish Rabbis teach on this verse, it is always in reference to a future Messiah who would not only have influence with the Jews but also would connect with the Gentiles. It is this one prophecy, above all others, that speaks to the Jewish people that Yeshua is the Messiah. Yeshua is the only Jew who has Gentile followers all over the globe, in every nation and in every language. We Gentiles are a fulfillment of this prophecy in Zechariah!

The act of grasping the tzitzit, which is on the corner of the garment, is a testament to coming under the authority of the one having the tzitzit. Zechariah is saying that it is the Gentiles who are coming under the authority of a Jew and going "with Him" because they hear that "God is with Him".

While the Gentiles did not fulfill this prophecy until after Yeshua was taken into Heaven, there were occasions where Jewish people reached out and touched the corner of His garment. By doing so, they came under the authority of this Jewish man. The immediate results of coming under authority of this man were astounding!

This brings us to a significant story in the New Testament. It is recorded in three of the Gospels. Obviously, these New Testament writers saw this as a very important event. Let's look at those three accounts.

Matthew 9:20-22

"And suddenly, a woman who had a flow of blood for twelve years came from behind and touched the hem of His garment. For she said to herself, "If only I may touch His garment, I shall be made well." But Jesus turned around, and when He saw her He said, "Be of good cheer, daughter; your faith has made you well." And the woman was made well from that hour."

Mark 5:25-34

"Now a certain woman had a flow of blood for twelve years, and had suffered many things from many physicians. She had spent all that she had and was no better, but rather grew worse. When she heard about Jesus, she

came behind Him in the crowd and touched His garment. For she said, "If only I may touch His clothes, I shall be made well."

Immediately the fountain of her blood was dried up, and she felt in her body that she was healed of the affliction. And Jesus, immediately knowing in Himself that power had gone out of Him, turned around in the crowd and said, "Who touched My clothes?"

But His disciples said to Him, "You see the multitude thronging You, and You say, "Who touched Me?"

And He looked around to see her who had done this thing. But the woman, fearing and trembling, knowing what had happened to her, came and fell down before Him and told Him the whole truth. And He said to her, "Daughter, your faith has made you well. Go in peace, and be healed of your affliction."

Luke 8:43-48

"Now a woman, having a flow of blood for twelve years, who had spent all her livelihood on physicians and could not be healed by any, came from behind and touched the border of His garment. And immediately her flow of blood stopped.

And Jesus said, "Who touched Me?"

When all denied it, Peter and those with him said, "Master, the multitudes throng and press You, and You say, "Who touched Me?"

But Jesus said, "Somebody touched Me, for I perceived power going out from Me." Now when the woman saw that she was not hidden, she came trembling; and falling down before Him, she declared to Him in the presence of all the people the reason she had touched Him and how she was healed immediately.

And He said to her, "Daughter, be of good cheer; your faith has made you well. Go in peace."

From these three accounts we can derive these points.

She had a flow of blood that made her ceremonial unclean. Being unclean she would not have been welcome into any group setting. In fact, she was required to announce "Unclean! Unclean" everywhere she went. Touching anyone would render that person ceremonially unclean. She was an outcast of society. No one wanted to be around her. I do not know how old she was when she began to have this problem, but I do know that for 12 long years she felt rejection.

She had spent all of her livelihood on physicians. She was in a hopeless financial condition.

The physicians could not help her. No treatment, medicine, or physical operation was ever successful during this 12-year period. She was a hopeless medical case.

This flow of blood certainly would have made her anemic, weak, and hardly able to walk. She steadily grew worse and worse in her condition.

Hopelessness was her only companion. Discouragement was her only friend. Depression was her daily lot.

In this hopeless, discouraged and depressed state, she heard of Jesus (Yeshua). No doubt she had heard about His healing and His teachings. She heard that people were saying that this might be the Messiah.

This message that she heard about Yeshua caused hope to suddenly arise. This hope came when all hope seemed lost. A simple message about the possibility of this man being the Messiah caused her to begin to have hope. Hope soon began to swell until faith was born. This hope that is turned into faith caused her to say something out loud, probably to everyone who would listen. "If I may but touch the hem of His garment, I shall be whole."

According to the Amplified Bible, she "kept saying" this. She repeated this over and over until it became a driving force. Although she was weak, penniless, rejected, and unwanted, she began a trip that she knew she was not allowed to be on. Even though she was unclean, she purposefully went toward the crowd where Yeshua was.

When she reached the location where Yeshua was, He had already passed her by. It seems that everything is going wrong for this woman. How on earth is she going to get close enough to Yeshua to touch the corner of his tallit? There are people all around Him. His own disciples have formed a protective circle around Him to keep the crowd from getting so close that they cut off the very air around Him. It looked impossible. It was impossible!

By now her words "If I may but touch the corner of His garment" have taken on an inner power that would not be denied. Not allowing herself to be discouraged, she came into the crowd of people surrounding Yeshua and began to crawl her way up to Him. Hands, knees, and feet are crawling on the dusty, rocky road.

As she is crawling, men are stepping on her already weak and frail body. The odor was sickening. Dirty men's feet who had walked over animal refuse came crushing down on her hands, arms, and legs. Yet, still she pressed on.

She only had one thing in mind. "If I may but touch the corner of His garment." The heat of the road and the heat of the bodies she was crawling through was stifling. Sweat poured from every pore mixing with the blood already flowing in copious amounts. She can barely move because of her weakness and because of all the obstacles in her way.

Finally, she is able to see the garment of Yeshua. She reaches out to grab the tzitzit that was dangling from the corner of the garment. Yeshua moves, someone kicks her in the face, and she misses her object. I can hear her mutter, "If I may but touch the hem of His garment".

Over and over she tries. Over and over she fails. Several attempts later, she suddenly touches the tzitzit. Immediately, she feels healing in her body. The blood stops flowing. Strength is surging through her. The bruises of the struggle are also gone. Even the smallest scratch is no longer there.

No sooner has she realized her wonderful healing, she hears Yeshua say, "Who touched me?"

Oh, no, she thought. Yeshua must be angry! I have made Him unclean. She tries to hide. She is afraid of what might happen to her. She is a woman among a group of men. Even without her disease, she shouldn't be here. Her history of rejection makes her fear rejection again. She expects rejection.

And then, His eyes capture hers. Her hair is disheveled. Her face and body are filthy from crawling on the road. She hardly is in a presentable appearance to speak to a Rabbi! She approaches Yeshua, ready for His condemnation. But she doesn't care now. Just to be healed has been worth all that she might endure.

She tells Yeshua everything. She tells him what she had heard about Him. She told Him about what she had said about touching the corner of His tallit. She told Him how she had almost missed Him entirely and how she had to crawl to get past the crowd that was surrounding Him. She told about touching His tzitzit and being healed the moment she touched it. Now she is ready for Him to condemn her for daring to bring her uncleanness into the group of men.

Something about His eyes, however, made her feel safe. Then she heard Him say to her, "Daughter…" He called her "Daughter". What could this mean? Was He offering His care and His protection as a Father would care and protect his own daughter? She had come for healing, but now He is offering her so much more! He wants to take her under His wing and provide for her. Not only is her physical need of healing been met, but now her financial needs are going to be met as well! But, oh that one word "Daughter". She is accepted! She is wanted! There in her filth He identifies her as a daughter!

A Rabbi's students were often called "sons", He identifies her as a student, a disciple. Oh how wonderful that one word was! All her insecurities are wiped away with just that one word!

No wonder that a later writer would say *"Behold what manner of love the Father has bestowed on us, that we should be called children of God!"* While still in our disheveled and filthy appearance He says to us, "Son", "Daughter". He takes you just as you are, but He does not leave you the way you are. Can you hear His voice speaking this one word to you today? You are accepted! You are loved! You are valued! All this because you have grasped the corner of "one who is a Jew" and said that you would "go with Him for you heard that God is with Him".

Yeshua continues speaking to her, *"Daughter, your faith has made you well"*. The word for well is the Greek word σωζω (sozo, pronounced sew'-zoh). The best definition I have found for this word is "restoration back to created function". It is wholeness in every area, physical, mental, spiritual, and material. When she touched the tzitzit on Yeshua's tallit, she got the whole package! She was restored back to where she should have been all along, back to her created function.

Then Yeshua adds "Go in peace". In Hebrew (which is what Yeshua would have been speaking to her, although the text was written in Greek) "peace" is שָׁלוֹם (shalom, pronounced shah'- lohm). Shalom means completeness, safety, soundness, welfare, health, prosperity, peace, quietness, tranquility, contentment, and friendship.

Through that one word "shalom", Yeshua encouraged her to go, (to continue) in the completeness, soundness, prosperity, and friendship that she received by touching His tzitzit on the corner of His garment. She was being encouraged to keep that which she had received and to not lose it. This meant to stay in shalom, stay in the liberty and the freedom wherein He had made her free and not be entangled again with the yoke of bondage.

You may be thinking that I have made a bit much out of the word "daughter" and its effect upon the woman. But I would like to offer to you where I would have gotten such an idea about how much the word "daughter" might have meant to her.

This woman's miracle was talked about everywhere. In fact, Mark 6:56 says this, *"Wherever He entered, into villages, cities, or the country, they laid the sick in the marketplaces, and begged Him that they might just touch the hem of His garment. And as many as touched Him were made well."* This woman became very well known. People who lived during this time could easily go to her hometown and look her up and see for themselves the miracle.

In fact, a historian of this period by the name of Eusebius visited Caesarea Philippi. While there he heard about this woman who had been healed by touching the tzitzit of Yeshua. This woman, as a sign of gratitude for her healing, had erected two brass figures at the gate of her house. Instead of depicting her reaching to touch the corner of

Yeshua's garment, she instead depicted the moment that Yeshua called her "daughter". She is shown on bended knee in supplication. The other figure is in the likeness of Yeshua, holding out His hand to help her. He had a double cloak of brass (the outer cloak would have been the tallit). Eusebius adds this explicit statement as to these figures. "They were in existence even in our day and we saw them with our own eyes when we stayed in the city."

The importance she placed on hearing Yeshua speak that word "daughter" is evident in the way the brass figures are designed. Obviously, she felt that this moment was even greater that the healing that she had received.

That is so true, even for us today. Our salvation and subsequent coming into a family relationship with Abba is far greater than any physical healing we may ever receive. It is true that He desires to heal us for He is Yahweh Rapha, The Lord our Healer. However, He wants to do so much more for us! He wants to restore us back to our created function in every area of our lives. He wants us to have restoration from the fall. All that Adam had lost He wants to give back to us. All we have to do is to reach out and grasp the corner of the garment and come under the authority of the man who is a Jew, Yeshua HaMaschiach (Jesus the Christ).

Chapter Fourteen
Final Scriptures With
The Prayer Shawl

The Rabbi's Yoke

Matthew 11:28-30 Come to Me, all you who labor and are heavy laden, and I will give you rest. Take My yoke upon you and learn from Me, for I am gentle and lowly in heart, and you will find rest for your souls. For My yoke is easy and My burden is light."

A Rabbi's teaching is commonly referred to as his "yoke". Because a Jewish Rabbi would teach the Torah to his disciples, the "yoke" would be the teaching of the Rabbi concerning the Torah. Since the tzitzit on a tallit serves to remind one of the Torah (through the presence of the 5 knots), the Rabbi's tallit then is also referred to as the "yoke".

Following a Rabbi is to "come under His yoke". This is representative of "coming under the Rabbi's tallit". When a Rabbi would call a disciple he would (as Elijah did to Elisha) cast his tallit over them and ask them to "follow me".

Therefore, when Yeshua said what He did in this verse, He was inviting you and me to come under his tallit and follow His teachings. He is inviting us to become His disciple.

Notice that He gives us a contrast to the "yoke" of the rest of Judaism. Other Jewish teachers and leaders caused you to "labor" and be "heavy laden" with rules too difficult to follow. Yeshua is "gentle and lowly (humble, not proud). He offers rest instead of labor. His "yoke is easy and His burden is light". The teaching of Yeshua, in contrast to other Jewish leaders, takes little effort and does not place undue burdens upon you.

We see what Yeshua was referring to as a contrast in this verse:

Matthew 23:1-5 "Then Jesus spoke to the multitudes and to His disciples, saying: "The scribes and the Pharisees sit in Moses' seat. Therefore, whatever they tell you to observe, that observe and do, but do not do according to their works; for they say, and do not do. For they bind heavy burdens, hard to bear, and lay them on men's shoulders; but they themselves will not move them with one of their fingers. But all their works they do to be seen by men. They make their phylacteries broad and enlarge the borders of their garments."

232

Look at what Yeshua says, *"For they bind heavy burdens, hard to bear, and lay them on men's shoulders"* (They lay a heavy yoke (tallit) on men's shoulders.)

His "yoke" is not the yoke of religion. His yoke is the yoke of relationship ("Come unto me"). As we come under His tallit, He teaches us, walks with us, and cares for us as no one else can.

If our walk with the Lord is hard and burdensome then it is more than likely that we have taken on the yoke of religiosity. Cast off the man-made garment of religion, take His garment on you! Be clothed today in His righteousness. Let His Spirit overwhelm you this very moment! His yoke is easy, and His burden is light!

The last part of the verse in Matt 23 above is another mention of the prayer shawl with the tzitzits. *"They make their phylacteries broad and enlarge the borders of their garments."*

Phylacteries is the Greek equivalent of the Hebrew word "tefillim". These are little black boxes that are affixed to the forehead and arm of a Jewish man. They contain a Scripture from the Torah. They wear these especially in prayer to fulfill the commandment to keep the Torah always between their eyes and upon their arms. The box on the head and the arm are connected by a leather strap that is wound in a prescribed manner.

The word "borders", that they enlarged, is the word kraspedon (κράσπεδον) in Greek. Kraspedon literally means corner. On the corner would be the tzitzit.

What Yeshua is saying is that the Scribes and the Pharisees were just making a show with the broad phylacteries and enlarged tzitzits. The tallit with the tzitzit speaks of authority. They thought that if they made the tzitzits long and broad that others would recognize that they had great authority. Yeshua did not say that it was wrong for them to have tzitzits, He simply was against trying to appear religious by showing off with them. Yeshua was looking at the heart and motives, not so much as what they were doing. They were guilty of doing the right thing in the wrong way.

The Folded Napkin

Another place in the New Testament where we see the mention of a prayer shawl is in John 20.

John 20:1-8 *"Now on the first day of the week Mary Magdalene went to the tomb early, while it was still dark, and saw that the stone had been taken away from the tomb. Then she ran and came to Simon Peter, and to the other disciple, whom Jesus loved, and said to them, "They have taken away the Lord out of the tomb, and we do not know where they have laid Him.*

Peter therefore went out, and the other disciple, and were going to the tomb. So they both ran together, and the other disciple outran Peter and came to the tomb first. And he, stooping down and looking in, saw the linen cloths lying there; yet he did not go in. Then Simon Peter came, following him, and went into the tomb; and he saw the linen cloths lying there, and the handkerchief that had been around His head, not lying with the linen cloths, but folded together in a place by itself. Then the other disciple, who came to the tomb first, went in also; and he saw and believed."

The word "handkerchief" (in the King James version, "napkin") certainly gives some readers a wrong picture of what was actually found folded by Peter and John. The Greek word for "handkerchief" is σουδάριον (soudarion, pronounced soo-dar'-ee-on). Since there is no Greek word for "tallit", this word comes closest to describing it. This word describes something much bigger than a handkerchief or napkin. This word actually means bandana or head scarf. It is unfortunate that the translators see it necessary to obfuscate any possible Jewish reference by misusing the meaning of the word.

Jewish burial customs include wrapping the person's prayer shawl around the head. Prior to placing the tallit around the head, they remove one of the tzitzit from a corner of the garment. It is the tzitzit that makes the garment a holy garment. Therefore, removing the tzitzit would make the prayer shawl a regular garment.

Since a deceased person no longer is under obligation to the mitzvahs (commandments) of the Torah, they no longer need a tzitzit to remind them of the requirements. Removing the tzitzit is a testament that only the living must be constantly reminded of the Torah.

Yeshua had been prepared for burial by Joseph of Arimathea and Nicodemus. The body of Yeshua was wrapped in a clean linen cloth. (Matthew 27:57-60, Mark 15:42-46, Luke 23:50-53, John 19:38-41). Some translations have wrongly re-worded John's text to read "strips of linen cloths" instead of a linen cloth.

The Jewish Misnah describes burial to be a wrapping of the body with a simple, linen shroud. Every one, rich or poor, are all buried the same. Even at death, every Jewish man are considered equals. As the color tekhelet had elevated everyone to being equally rich while alive, so the linen shroud made everyone equally poor at death.

Jewish men and women are buried without jewelry, makeup, or anything pertaining to their status or wealth. Even venerable Rabbis are buried the same as the common fisherman. Yeshua was no exception. Though He was buried in a rich man's tomb, He was buried just like every deceased Israelite.

We see then that "handkerchief" is in reality a tallit with the tzitzit cut off one corner. The "linen cloths" are actually the burial shroud.

We see a similar description of burial customs in the raising of Lazarus.

John 11:43-44 Now when He had said these things, He cried with a loud voice, "Lazarus, come forth! "And he who had died came out bound hand and foot with graveclothes, and his face was wrapped with a cloth. Jesus said to them, "Loose him, and let him go."

The graveclothes of Lazarus would be the burial shroud or linen cloth. The cloth wrapped around his face would be the prayer shawl with a corner removed.

There are striking differences in the resurrection of Lazarus and the resurrection of Yeshua. With Lazarus, someone had to remove the graveclothes and the tallit that he was wrapped in. With Yeshua, the shroud and the tallit remained wrapped while the body of Yeshua simply passed through the cloth.

When Peter and John went into the sepulcher and saw not only the shroud but also the tallit still in the same shape as if still wrapped around a body but without a body, they saw and believed. The Greek for the word "saw" literally means that they gazed intently. It took a moment for the realization of what had just occurred to sink in.

After some reflection, they understood that no one would have removed the body and left the graveclothes and the tallit intact. They had to realize at that point that Yeshua had indeed risen, though they as of yet had not seen him.

The translation that the tallit around his head was folded is unfortunate. The word for folded in Greek is entulisso (ἐντυλίσσω) and should be translated, "wrapped". This word only occurs three times in the New Testament.

Matthew 27:59: *"had taken the body, **he wrapped** it in a clean linen cloth,"*
Luke 23:53: *"And he took it down, **and wrapped** it in linen, and laid"*
John 20:7: *"the linen clothes, but **wrapped together** in a place by itself."*

By this we can understand that the tallit was wrapped as if still around the head of Yeshua. However, there was no body within the wrapping.

The prayer shawl, therefore, plays an extremely important part not only in the life but also in the death, burial, and resurrection of our Lord and Savior. At the end of this book we will discover that the tallit will continue to be identified with Yeshua. We have one more event where Yeshua will once again don His tallit. The tallit is important to our Savior. Perhaps it should be important to us as well.

Unusual Miracles, Tent Making, Lydia, and Selling Garments

Another possible mention of the tallit is in the following verse.

Acts 19:11-12 *"Now God worked unusual miracles by the hands of Paul, so that even handkerchiefs or aprons were brought from his body to the sick, and the diseases left them and the evil spirits went out of them."*

The word for handkerchief is the same Greek word used for handkerchief in the account of Peter and John in the tomb of the risen

Christ. It is evident that it was prayer shawls that was taken from Paul after his wearing them that brought healing to the sick and diseased as well as deliverance from evil spirits.

This is extremely probable because Paul was a tent maker by trade. Since the Jewish people as well as the Romans of that period lived in homes, it is extremely unlikely that Paul could have made a living from making tents. This is especially clear when you consider how long it takes to make one tent. It hardly would have been a source of quick income.

However, if Paul made "little tents" which is what the word tallit actually means, he would have had a ready source of income any time he needed it. We know that he was a student of Gamaliel at one time in his life. As a student, it would be customary for him to make and sell tallits to support himself and his schooling.

Acts 18:1-3 *"After these things Paul departed from Athens and went to Corinth. And he found a certain Jew named Aquila, born in Pontus, who had recently come from Italy with his wife Priscilla (because Claudius had commanded all the Jews to depart from Rome); and he came to them. So, because he was of the same trade, he stayed with them and worked; for by occupation they were tentmakers."*

Not only did Paul make tallits to support himself, he also would have had a perfect connection to spread the Gospel. When Paul had his vision to go to Macedonia, he first encounters Lydia, a seller of purple from Thyatira.

Acts 16: 14-15 *"Now a certain woman named Lydia heard us. She was a seller of purple from the city of Thyatira, who worshiped God. The Lord opened her heart to heed the things spoken by Paul. And when she and her household were baptized, she begged us, saying, "If you have judged me to be faithful to the Lord, come to my house and stay." So she persuaded us."*

Thyatira was about 300 miles from Philippi. How Lydia came to be living here so far from her town we do not know. Thyatira was a prominent city for the dye industry. The purple dye was taken from the murex trunculus snail and was used for wealthy and powerful individuals for their clothing. This dye would be the tekhelet that I wrote about in a previous chapter.

That being the case, Lydia would have been a very wealthy person. The cost of tekhelet was 20 times the value of the same amount of gold! She would probably have a large work force who would extract the dye that she would then travel from place to place to sell.

Since Paul made tallits, he would have a natural opportunity to relate to Lydia. I am sure they had a conversation about tekhelet and perhaps Paul may have purchased some dye for future tallits that he would make. In the process, Lydia becomes interested in the message that Paul speaks and is converted and baptized. It is interesting that there is a church begun at Thyatira and is one of the seven churches in Revelation.

Lydia is the first convert in Macedonia and her conversion must have caused quite a stir. Everyone would know of her, because everyone would have the servant string of their tzitzits dyed in this purple dye. For such a wealthy and well-known person to become converted would be the talk of the town.

The incredible value of this particular dye makes two New Testament Scriptures take on a deeper meaning. The tallit with its strings of blue on each corner would be a garment of value. It would be, most likely, the most expensive garment you might own. Look at this Scripture.

Luke 22:36 *"Then He said to them, "But now, he who has a money bag, let him take it, and likewise a knapsack; and he who has no sword, let him sell his garment and buy one."*

For Yeshua to suggest that a person could sell his garment and buy a sword indicates that the garment in question must be valuable enough to sell. The tallit would definitely be valuable enough. The tallit would also be a garment that others would want even if it was used. A well cared for tallit would not lose its value over time.

The Sheet From Heaven

Acts 10:9-20 The next day, as they went on their journey and drew near the city, Peter went up on the housetop to pray, about the sixth hour. Then he became very hungry and wanted to eat; but while they made ready, he fell into a trance and saw heaven opened and an object like a great sheet bound at the four corners, descending to him and let down to the earth. In it were all kinds of four-footed animals of the earth, wild beasts, creeping things, and birds of the air. And a voice came to him, "Rise, Peter; kill and eat."

But Peter said, "Not so, Lord! For I have never eaten anything common or unclean."

And a voice spoke to him again the second time, "What God has cleansed you must not call common." This was done three times. And the object was taken up into heaven again.

Now while Peter wondered within himself what this vision which he had seen meant, behold, the men who had been sent from Cornelius had made inquiry for Simon's house, and stood before the gate. And they called and asked whether Simon, whose surname was Peter, was lodging there.

While Peter thought about the vision, the Spirit said to him, "Behold, three men are seeking you. Arise therefore, go down and go with them, doubting nothing; for I have sent them."

Acts 11:1-18 Now the apostles and brethren who were in Judea heard that the Gentiles had also received the word of God. And when Peter came up to Jerusalem, those of the circumcision contended with him, saying, "You went in to uncircumcised men and ate with them!"

But Peter explained it to them in order from the beginning, saying: "I was in the city of Joppa praying; and in a trance I saw a vision, an object descending like a great sheet, let down from heaven by four corners; and it came to me. When I observed it intently and considered, I saw four-footed animals of the earth, wild beasts, creeping things, and birds of the air. And I heard a voice saying to me, "Rise, Peter; kill and eat." But I said, "Not so, Lord! For nothing common or unclean has at any time entered my mouth." But the voice answered me again from heaven, "What God has cleansed you must not call common." Now this was done three times, and all were drawn up again into heaven. At that very moment, three men stood before the house where I was, having been sent to me from Caesarea. Then the Spirit told me to go with them, doubting nothing. Moreover, these six brethren accompanied me, and we entered the man's house. And he told us how he had seen an angel standing in his house, who said to him, "Send men to Joppa, and call for Simon whose surname is Peter, who will tell you words by which you and all your household will be saved." And as I began to speak, the Holy Spirit fell upon them, as upon us at the beginning. Then I remembered the word of the Lord, how He said, "John indeed baptized with water, but you shall be baptized with the Holy Spirit." If therefore God gave them the same gift as He gave us when we believed on the Lord Jesus Christ, who was I that I could withstand God?"

When they heard these things they became silent; and they glorified God, saying, "Then God has also granted to the Gentiles repentance to life."

Peter went up to the rooftop to pray. As Jewish men still do today, he would put his prayer shawl over his head. While under the tallit, in his personal Holy of Holies, he would begin to rock back and forth. This would produce a trance-like state that helps one to concentrate upon God.

While in this trance, he sees a vision. There is a large sheet let down from heaven by its four corners. The sheet would have no meaning to Peter except for the mention of the four corners. As we shall see this must have been a very large tallit that was lowered by its four tzitzits on the corners.

Inside this sheet (this tallit) was all kinds of unclean animals. We will find by reading the rest of the story that these animals are simply representative of Gentiles. God is showing Peter, through unclean animals wrapped in a holy garment (a tallit), that He is bringing the Gentiles into a holy relationship. God is demonstrating to Peter that Gentiles have a right to the teachings held within the prayer shawl.

Peter comes out of his trance and subsequently goes with men who lead him to Cornelius' house. Cornelius and his whole household believe Peter's message and are baptized with the Holy Ghost. This becomes the first Gentile church.

Those of us who were *"aliens from the commonwealth of Israel and strangers from the covenants of promise,"* (Ephesians 2:12). Now we *"who once were far off have been brought near by the blood of Christ."* (Ephesians 2:13).

When we Gentiles are born again we are brought into the commonwealth of Israel, we should become acquainted with the covenants of promise. We have been united, Jew and Gentile, into one body. In Christ, we have been made "one new man".

We are not separate from Israel. God has not forgot His people. I long for the day when the wall of separation that the Gentiles have erected between Jewish believers in Yeshua and Gentile believers in Yeshua will be taken down. It took a Heavenly vision to influence Peter to reach out to Gentiles. Perhaps we Gentiles are in need of a Heavenly vision like his today.

He Is Coming!

Revelation 19:11-16 *"Now I saw heaven opened, and behold, a white horse. And He who sat on him was called Faithful and True, and in righteousness He judges and makes war. His eyes were like a flame of fire, and on His head were many crowns. He had a name written that no one knew except Himself. He was clothed with a robe dipped in blood, and His name is called The Word of God. And the armies in heaven, clothed in fine linen, white and clean, followed Him on white horses. Now out of His mouth goes a sharp sword, that with it He should strike the nations. And He Himself will rule them with a rod of iron. He Himself treads the winepress of the fierceness and wrath of Almighty God. And He has on His robe and on His thigh a name written:*

KING OF KINGS AND
LORD OF LORDS."

We end this book with a final reference to the prayer shawl. Yeshua, who was born a Jew, circumcised the eighth day as a Jew, grew up Torah observant throughout His life, was crucified as a Jew, buried as a Jew, rose from the grave as a Jew, appeared to His disciples as a Jew, ascended into Heaven as a Jew, now is coming back to earth as a Jew! Here in this glorious passage we see Yeshua with His prayer shawl over His shoulders with the tzitzit on His thigh, coming to set up His Kingdom on this earth for 1000 years.

This passage begins with *"Now I saw heaven opened"*. This was not the first time heaven was open. In Revelation 4:1 A door was open in heaven and John was invited to "come up" into heaven. This pictures the rapture of the church. This is a prelude to the Marriage

Supper of the Lamb. For seven years we are in the Chuppah with our Lord and Savior consummating the long awaited marriage. During those same seven years the earth has had the Great Tribulation. The Anti-Christ and the False Prophet have taken over the earth. Now heaven opens again.

This time heaven is not open for us to come up, heaven is opened for us to come down! Here we are in white robes, the armies of God, following our Leader who is on a white horse! He is Yahweh Sabaoth (The LORD of Hosts).

We are coming out of the Chuppah for the party! If you continue reading you will find there is an invitation to a great supper of our God. Only, it is the birds of the air who receive this invitation. They are invited to come to eat the flesh of those who are making war with us. This language is much like what David said to Goliath. It is war language!

I Samuel 17:45-46 *"Then David said to the Philistine, "You come to me with a sword, with a spear, and with a javelin. But I come to you in the name of the LORD of hosts, the God of the armies of Israel, whom you have defied. This day the LORD will deliver you into my hand, and I will strike you and take your head from you. And this day I will give the carcasses of the camp of the Philistines to the birds of the air and the wild beasts of the earth, that all the earth may know that there is a God in Israel."*

The part that I want to focus on is the tallit and the tzitzit that Yeshua is wearing. Much can be said about the three mentions of His Name (one where no one knows the name) as well as the sword and other wonderful pictures within this passage. However, I want to stay (as much as possible) within the confines of the subject matter of this book.

"He was clothed with a robe dipped in blood". The word translated "robe" is the Greek word ἱμάτιον (pronounced hih-mah'-tee-on). This Greek word most often is translated "mantle". The Greek word for "clothed" is περιβαλλο (pronounced per-ee-bal'-loh). This word means to wrap around, ballo (thrown or wrap) and peri (around). With this

description, we can see that the Greek is trying describe a Hebrew mantle which is wrapped around a person like a shawl.

This "robe" (mantle) has a name on it that extends to Yeshua's thigh. With Yeshua riding on a horse, the mantle (or shawl) would have this name on something that would come over His thigh. With what we know about tzitzit and how it can be tied to represent words, it can easily be seen that this is what this is speaking about.

Yeshua left His disciples and gave a priestly blessing over them as He ascended. Now, as He is coming back, to ultimately place His foot on the Mount of Olives once again, he is dressed in His Jewish garment, the prayer shawl. On the corners of this tallit is the tzitzit proclaiming that He is King of kings and Lord of lords.

During the next 1000 years He will reign from Jerusalem and the whole earth will come to Jerusalem to celebrate the Feast of Tabernacles (Zechariah 14:16-21). We will join in with the Jewish people who have believed in Yeshua HaMaschiah and as "one new man" we will celebrate the Feasts.

Since this is a prophecy that will be fulfilled, should we not search out, in order to understand, the Jewish roots of our faith? Easter Sunday is nice, but Passover is when Yeshua was crucified, the Feast of Unleavened Bread is when He was buried, and the Feast of First Fruits is when Yeshua rose from the grave. Shavuot, the Feast of Weeks, is when the Holy Spirit fell in the Upper Room 50 days after Passover. The Feast of Trumpets is the rapture of the Church. The Day of Atonement is the Great White Throne Judgment! The Feast of Tabernacles is the 1000-year reign of Christ.

There is an increasing interest within the church to search the Jewish roots of our faith. I do not believe that this is coincidental. I believe Yeshua, our Savior, is beginning to prepare us to be united once again with our Jewish brethren, just as we were in the book of Acts. It is obvious that we will be together in Heaven and in the millennium. Why not reach out for unity with the Jewish people now?

If you have not purchased a prayer shawl as of yet, you really should consider getting one. There is a vast wealth of knowledge that I have only begun to tap into. As you pray under your personal tallit, your Holy of Holies, I am sure that you will experience the presence of the Holy Spirit in a way you have never felt before. It really is awesome to pray under the prayer shawl. After all, the prayer shawl was not given only to the Jewish people, it is our teaching tool sent by God as well.

May God bless you as you learn more of Him.

67473476R00137

Made in the USA
Charleston, SC
13 February 2017